Another Cornish Beaside Book

Another Cornish Bedside Book

Dr D. Selleck Ph.D., M.A.

DYLLANSOW TRURAN

Published 1992

Copyright © 1992

ISBN 1 85022 0301

Typeset by Kestrel Data, Exeter
Printed and bound in Great Britain by Short Run Press Ltd, Exeter

Contents

Foreword

The injunction in The Book Of Common Prayer, to 'read, mark, learn, and inwardly digest,' may well have been addressed to all local historians. It is their function to do just that, and despite the inevitable condensations to preserve the essential flavour.

Confronted with the rich seams of historical material, which, in Cornwall, are the accumulated records of a nation rather than a county, one can only hope to have done one's 'digging' in the right places.

It is the life and experiences of the individual (famous or obscure) its joys and sorrows, its drama, and its humour that gives us the most vivid glimpses of the past. I hope the biographical sketches, and the examples of past generations of Cornish folk at home, work, or play, will have the same fascination for the reader as they have for me.

Our most distant past is however not accessible in the same way. It is through the 'folk memory' of ancient customs and celebrations that we are linked with the long gone generations. Perhaps the closest we get to them is when we walk in their very footsteps to where, in stone, the imaginative work of their hands in turn stimulates our imagination.

That is why, as a tribute to our Celtic heritage, I have included the chapter on holy wells and the buildings associated with them. The beautiful drawings of the pre-photographic era have preserved much that has, in the last century, disappeared, and illustrate for us the success or otherwise of 'restoration.'

This Bal Tonight

Cold is this bal tonight,
It no longer has a roof to cover it.
Quiet is this bal tonight,
It no longer has an engine to warm it.
Lonely is this bal tonight,
It no longer has men within it.
Dark is this bal tonight,
It no longer has candles to light it.
Dead is this bal tonight,
The miners have gone,
And it's shafts are empty

Perran Tauran – 1990 – aged 12
('Bal' = 'mine' in Cornish)

Deadwood Dick—Cornish Hero

Cornwall has its folk heroes, from King Arthur to Trelawny, yet there is one of her sons, known for his exploits—real or imaginary throughout the English-speaking world, though strangely un-celebrated in his native country. His real name will be totally unfamiliar, but his nickname, 'Deadwood Dick', rings an instant bell.

Richard Bullock was born at Ruthros, near St. Columb, on 20th August, 1847. His father John Bullock was foreman of a clay-works at Retew, in the St. Austell area, as such he had the customary title of 'Captain', and his five sons, all well-built lads, naturally worked under him. The whole family worshipped together as well, at Queens United Methodist Free Church. Richard as a boy and young man was a member of the choir.

Life with the Bullock family was not all work and chapel, their favourite sport was shooting. Richard (or Dick as he was usually called) was fascinated by pigeon shooting, at eighteen he was already a crack shot. His friend Ned Hocking of Fraddon, told the story of their first pigeon shooting match, at St. Stephen-in-Brannel 'Feast Week'. On their way to the match, Dick told a roadman they met that they would show him the first and second prizes on their way back, and they did just that. The story was often told of how Dick's dog flushed out four partridges, two of which flew left and two right, and how he got two with one barrel and the other pair with a second barrel.

Dick married a local girl, Susie Poad. At an early morning Christmas Day service, in 1873, he caused some amusement in chapel by singing as a chorister 'Unto us a child is born', for his son Maurice had been born a few days previously. No fortune

Deadwood Dick (Richard Bullock)

could be made as a Victorian clay-labourer, in fact hardly a living for a family, and Dick, as so many other Cornish miners, decided to face long years of separation from his wife and baby son and sail to an American 'El-Dorado', in his case located in the Black Hills of South Dakota, mining not for clay or tin, but gold.

As other hard-working miners, he became exasperated by the regularity with which the stage-coaches that took the gold away were held up and robbed. He decided to do something about it and, exchanging shovel for six-shooter, volunteered as a bullion guard, for the Homestake Mine, then owned by Senator George Hearst, the father of William Randolph Hearst who at this time was beginning to build his newspaper empire.

The gold was carried in the Deadwood Stage (famed in story and song) along the perilous route from Cheyenne to Deadwood via Laramie. It ran through Buffalo Gap, Lame Johnny Creek, Red Canyon and Squaw Gap, all notorious haunts of bandits such as Peg Leg Bradley, Dunk Blackburn, and Curly Grimes, not to mention the Sioux Indians. In its time it carried such fabulous passengers as Calamity Jane, Wild Bill Hickock, and Buffalo Bill. The coach itself was later acquired by Buffalo Bill for the 'Wild-West Show' with which he toured the world. It was a handsome vehicle, though of course very strongly built to run on the atrocious tracks that served as roads in the west. It had a red painted body, yellow wheels, and each door had a handsome picture of a landscape. It carried nine persons inside and eight outside. It sounds incongruous to say that they travelled to Deadwood on the 'Concord', but this was the name of the coach (from its place of manufacture in New Hampshire).

The bandits must have rued the day, in 1882, that Dick started riding shotgun. The notorious Lame Johnny for one tried to hold up the coach, but never made it back to his creek. When, at Hurricane Flats, he coolly stepped out into the road, pistols in hand, Dick dropped him in his tracks. His quick shooting soon earned him the name of 'Deadwood Dick' and he became under that name the subject of local newspaper reports. Although he enclosed these cuttings in letters home to Cornwall, he was not a great writer and said little about his part in the stories. Guns and sporting dogs were the main subjects of letters to his father and Ned Hocking. The Methodist choirboy, who had now proved his skill in shooting bandits as well as partridges, acquired a taste for the job and left the Homestake Mine job to battle with the 'baddies' as official or unofficial lawman wherever in the west his services were required.

It was now that he became quite literally 'a legend in his own lifetime'. Educational progress in America, as in Europe, had produced newly literate millions to be entertained by the written word. So sprang up the 'Dime Novel', selling at ten cents apiece to hundreds of thousands of people who normally could not afford books at all. Author Edward L. Wheeler, having seen the newspaper reports, made Deadwood Dick the subject of one of them, the book sold well and from now on imagination and invention made him into a character, if not larger than, very different from life.

Thus began the still unending avalanche of 'pulp' Westerns, and it is amazing how constantly the characters and places in them are those of South Dakota, in Dick Bullock's time there. When first the silent films came, and then the talkies, these provided the basis of hundreds of films and many songs, a standard example being 'The Deadwood Stage'.

Unlike Calamity Jane and Wild Bill Hickock, and other characters from that era, whose graves (timely or otherwise) are an attraction to tourists in the Deadwood Cemetery today, Dick Bullock spent his last years in the company of a couple of other 'Homestake' bullion guards, Herbert Eakin and W. R. Dickinson, at Thorncroft Sanatorium, Glendale, California, probably, one guesses, being maintained there by Mr. Hearst. There he died peacefully in his bed at the age of 73, in 1921. So close to Hollywood, where his celluloid ghosts rode on, so far from Cornwall, where his family still lived in the world of china-clay and chapel he had known half a century before.

John Opie
The Wondrous Cornishman

From the mid 18th to the mid 19th Century, there was, in Cornwall and Devon, an unparalleled flowering of artistic talent. The Royal Academy echoed to westcountry accents. Reynolds of Plympton; Northcote, Haydon, and Eastlake of Plymouth; and the enameller Bone from Truro; all were successful professional painters. There were also first rate amateurs, such as Sir William Elford, Recorder of Plymouth, and his friend Richard Phillips of the Redruth mining family. Yet another amateur painter in this circle was Dr. Wolcot at Truro, physician, sometime clergyman, and, as 'Peter Pindar', a witty, sharp tongued satirical poet. Falstaffian in inclination and appearance, he had a large circle of enemies, and some remarkable friends, including William Cookworthy, the Quaker chemist who discovered china-clay in Cornwall, and made, at Plymouth, the first true English porcelain, and was himself no mean hand with a brush.

A successful and fashionable portraitist was able, in that prephotographic era, to make a fortune by recording for future generations, the features of the wealthy and their families. This fact did not escape the acquisitive Wolcot, an ardent admirer of Reynolds, and a friend of Northcote, his dream was to discover a new Reynolds, or at least someone who would approach Sir Joshua's earning capacity, in whose artistic and financial success he might share.

In part at least, his dream came true, when, in 1775, he found John Opie of St. Agnes. This fourteen year old son of a mine carpenter was already a village celebrity, and by no means the

John Opie

Dr. John Wolcot

illiterate oaf of later legend. Retrospective claims of 'gentle' descent have been made for both sides of Opie's family, but living in their 'one up one down' thatched cottage, now the tourist-attracting 'Harmony Cottage' (but originally known as 'Blowing House', as it had been adapted from a mining installation) they were certainly just ordinary working folk, in frugal, but not poverty-stricken, circumstances.

John, the baby of the family (his mother was forty eight when he was born) could be afforded at least some basic education at the, unusually good, village school. Here he showed his high intelligence and application, by making rapid progress in Arithmetic and Euclid. At only twelve years old, he demonstrated remarkable self confidence by starting an evening school for the poor of St. Agnes. Some pupils were nearly twice his age. Proud of his mathematical skill, his uncle dubbed him 'the young Sir Isaac', but his consuming passion was to paint. He would often start at first light, and the cottage walls were decorated with portraits of family and friends.

His sister worked for a local family called Nankivell, and John one day crept quietly into the hall of their mansion to gaze enraptured at an oil painting of a farmyard, which he afterwards copied so successfully that it was sold for five shillings, to the local vicar. Wolcot was asked to come to see the prodigy, and, watching him at work on a drawing of old Mrs. Nankivell's cat, 'cried out in rapture "EUREKA!" and foretold the future destinies of the lad with all the enthusiasms of a prophet, and from that instance afforded him every possible assistance.' The doctor, aided by John's mother, persuaded his father to let him give up the 'safe' prospect of carpentering, and go to live with him at Truro.

Here, he not only educated him in artistic skills, but taught him to read and write well, in English and in French, as a preparation for his career. He had also to learn the social graces, so as 'not to pick his teeth with his fork at dinnertime, nor at breakfast to clap his "vingers" in the sugar basin.' Wolcot also insisted that he raised his fee for a portrait, from the usual seven and sixpence to half a guinea. Business was good, many Cornish country houses acquired early 'Opies'. A patron also commissioned him to paint Cornish 'characters', among them, at the end of her life, Dolly Pentreath, the fishwife who was the last native speaker of the Cornish language. Elated by the 'fortune' he was making, John, on a visit home, threw thirty guineas onto the cottage floor, and rolling on it in his new clothes, cried 'look mother I'm walving (wallowing) in gold.'

There is no basis for the hints of Wolcot's enemies that there was a homosexual relationship between him and Opie. John was a quite normal youth, and there is a story that he once forestalled Wolcot's attentions to a young lady, by 'borrowing' his horse to visit her himself. Opie painted a picture of one of his village sweethearts, Mary James, milking her cow.

Wolcot decided that Opie, at nineteen, was ready to be launched into the real artistic world, and they made their way to London. They paused in Plymouth, to paint the only picture of the aged William Cookworthy, it now presides over his lovely porcelain, in Plymouth Art Gallery. They obtained some other commissions in Exeter.

In London, Opie was presented by Wolcot as a primitive genius, the 'wild animal of St. Agnes, caught among the tin works.' He appeared at first almost like a circus freak, with green feathers stuck in his hair, and it was claimed that he had never even seen an 'old master.' Wolcot had good connections to supplement the showmanship, and after he had got Opie into the Palace itself, where George III congratulated him and bought a picture, he began to be accepted in the best circles. His success was a blow to Northcote, who felt betrayed by Wolcot and said: 'Wolcot was puffing him off as a prodigy, as an inspired genius found in a tin mine in Cornwall. The great world flocked about him, so that the street where he lived was scarcely passable . . . Opie was a dreadful hurt to me at this time.' Wolcot did not literally sing his protegés praises, but, in 1782, he put them into verse:

> Speak muse, who formed that matchless head?
> The Cornish boy in tin mines bred,
> Whose native genius like his diamonds shone,
> In secret, till chance gave him to the sun.

Opie, despite Wolcot's tutoring, and his own diligent self-education (he knew much of Milton and of Shakespeare by heart) remained a 'rough diamond'. He was good natured, and tolerant to a fault, but his use of a few terse words to convey the blunt truth, though it amused King George, could startle the society in which he now moved.

Wolcot and Opie had made a written agreement on a 'fifty-fifty' sharing of profits. This lasted for a year, when, said Wolcot, 'my pupil told me that I might return to the country, as he could now do for himself.' They remained on friendly enough terms, but were never as close. Opie's only cryptic comment, when it was suggested that he was ungrateful to Wolcot, was 'Ay—in time you will know him.' There was also the fact that John, now twenty one years of age, had fallen in love with one of his sitters, a black eyed beauty called Mary Bunn, a solicitor's daughter. In 1782, they were married at St. Martin's-in-the-Fields. The lady, to coin a phrase, was no lady! Cyrus Redding, the gossipy, Plymouth newspaperman recalled how a 'handsome young relative' of his, 'on whose arm she was leaning' as, with her husband just out of earshot, they were passing through Soho Square, had his attention directed by her to 'a certain notorious house', with the comment that it was a curious place and she would like to see inside it some day, if he would show it to her. The marriage did last thirteen years, but in 1795 Mary ran off with another man. Opie was, by now, well enough connected to obtain a Parliamentary Act of Divorce, a difficult and expensive process. Later, passing St. Martin's, with an atheist friend who remarked that he was christened there, he wryly observed 'I was married in it, they make unsure work there, for it neither holds in wedlock nor in baptism.'

Opie never had any children, but was by no means alone in the world, he maintained close ties with his family. Like Reynolds, he never lacked a capable sister to give domestic support. His father, for whom he anxiously enquired in letters home, died early, but his mother lived to ninety-five to enjoy his success. In any case his days were filled with incessant painting. Eight hundred of his works are catalogued, more than one hundred and forty were Academy exhibits. As well as portraits, he specialised in historical subjects. One of them was of the assassination of James I of Scotland. This, with 'The Assassination of David Rizzio' was bought to hang in the City Gallery, at London's Guildhall.

In 1798, Opie married Amelia Alderson, the twenty-nine year old daughter of a Norwich physician. They proved to be well suited. She was a talented writer and published poems and novels. After Opie died she became a Quaker and wrote many moral tracts. A strong feminist, she was a friend of one of her husband's most remarkable 'subjects', Mary Wollstonecroft, a literary lady and radical politician, who, like her son-in-law, Shelley, anticipated (by a couple of centuries) the permissive society. In 1802, Opie and his wife went to Paris, to view the scores of priceless pictures looted by Napoleon from other European capitals.

Opies reputation grew steadily, in 1805 he was elected professor of painting to the Royal Academy and did a great deal of extra work, preparing the lectures he commenced to deliver in February 1807. This was the high point of his career, but, in April of the same year, he was the victim of a mysterious illness, attributed by some to lead absorbed from the paints he used, but undoubtedly aggravated by overwork. Despite the attentions of six doctors, and the devoted nursing of his wife, and his sister, he died. His prophecy to his sister, 'Aye girl, I too shall be buried in St. Paul's,' was fulfilled.

He was laid, with due pomp, alongside Sir Joshua Reynolds. Opie's unsophisticated character, reflected in his direct and uncluttered style, makes comparison with the polished grace of Reynolds difficult, but to Reynolds we will give the last word. As soon as he first saw his work, he had enthused to Northcote on 'a wondrous Cornishman, who is carrying all before him. He is Caravaggio and Velasquez in one!' Such praise, from such a quarter, is conclusive.

Christmas Eve at The Jamaica Inn

Before the publication, in 1936, of Miss Du Maurier's highly dramatic novel, Jamaica Inn, on Bodmin Moor, was no better known than any of the once busy hostelries which were, until the railway came, stopping points for the London mail coaches, on the Exeter to Falmouth run. Baring-Gould tells us that later it was 'converted into a temperance house, was far from clean, harboured innumerable fleas, and did little business.'

For a long time before this sad decline however, it had gone on serving refreshment (alcoholic or otherwise) to the local farmers and any travellers still using horsepower to get to destinations unserved by either the Southern, or Great Western railways. Possibly the occasional uncustomed barrel got into the cellar, even maybe of Jamaica rum, but there was none of the melodramatic mayhem of the novelist's imagination.

We have, in the recollections of one traveller, an amusing story of a Christmas Eve, spent under the hospitable roof. He was John Burton a young china salesman going the rounds of the village shops with wares from his father's Bodmin business. He says: 'I well remember the 24th. December, 1853, myself and brother Joe (who afterwards became a well-known auctioneer) rose at 5 o'clock in the morning, fed the horse, and made a start at 5.45 a.m. with a wagon load of goods. The morning was dark, and when we came to Callywith turnpike gate it was closed. We knocked Henry Mark, the toll-keeper, up to let us through. He looked out of the window and at first refused to let us pass until daylight. We told him that we would unhang the gate and pass through without paying the toll. This fetched the old man down, with his long coat, and knitted night cap, with horn lantern in

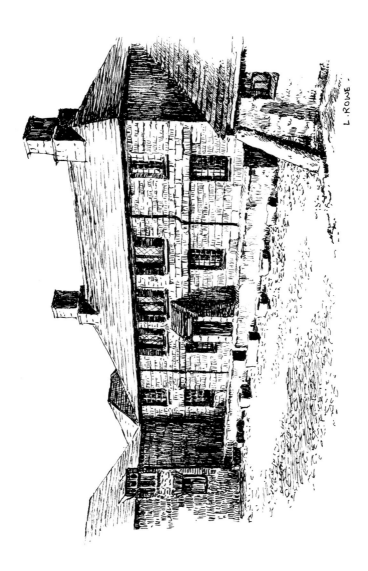

JAMAICA INN, BOLVENTOR

L. ROWE.

Jamaica Inn

his hand. He opened the gate and told us that we ought to be poisoned for breaking a man's rest. Having delivered the goods, and fairly on the way home, we stopped at the Jamaica Inn, where the old mail coaches used to change their horses, to feed our horse, not forgetting ourselves. After giving old Dapper his feed of oats, we went into the inn kitchen, where we ordered a hot meal. The landlady asked what we would like, and suggested a hot squab pie, which she took out of a huge kitchen range well loaded with burning turf, the odour of which increased our appetite considerably. We polished off the pie and pocketed the crust to eat on the moors when homeward bound. When the landlady came in and saw that we had finished the pie, she looked with amazement at us and declared, "Why, drat you boys, whativer have 'ee done with the pie?" We answered, "Why, ate'n missus. Do'y think us called the horse in to help us, or what?" She smartly answered, "I should 'a thought you had the Bodmin Militia here to help 'ee out. I never seed such gluttons in my life." '

When the Burtons asked what they had to pay, they got the recipe for a squab pie thrown in:

'Sixpence for the crust, threepence for the suet, nine pence for the giblets, eightpence for apples, onions, spice, currants and sugar, and fourpence for baking 'en.' She added fourpence for two 'dishes of tay,' and said it would be two and eightpence altogether. When the boys had paid, she asked, by way of ridicule, if they could eat any more. They, responding, stuffed down some carroway seed buns, after being refused a slice of next day's Christmas cake!

The boys, whose father was a strict teetotaller, did not dare to match their eating with the same amount of drinking, but as the moormen and farmers drifted in to pass a convivial evening around the roaring fire, while the wind howled across the moor outside, they joined in the party spirit, as songs were sung, often about the highwaymen who once infested such lonely stretches of road. Naturally however they wanted to be home in Bodmin before Christmas morning, so they left before the rest of the company.

They carried a passenger with them on the cart, one Billy Peppermint, a local 'character', who lived in Bodmin. He had had far too much liquid refreshment to want a share in the purloined pie-crust, as they jogged along. He was, in modern terms 'legless.' When they reached Bodmin, they got him off the cart and propped him up against the iron railings of a house. Just then, a party of carol singers came along. As they sang 'While shepherds watched their flocks by night,' Billy accompanied them, but he was still back at Jamaica Inn with the Highwayman ballad, and roared out: 'When I am dead they'll say the truth, I was a wild and wicked youth.' He then slid gently to the ground, and if the waits had continued with 'Christians awake, salute the happy morn,' it would have had no results with him much before mid day.

The Burton boys, no doubt, went home and stabled 'Dapper' as quietly as possible, in order to get off to bed without explaining exactly where they had spent the evening to their father.

Cornwall's Captain Courageous

*From the cradle to the grave adventurer, buccaneer,
entrepreneur and member of Parliament James Silk
Buckingham was a figure larger than life*

James Silk Buckingham was born at Flushing, Falmouth, in
1786, and he was an adventurer almost as soon as he left the
cradle.

He loved to roam the harbour's wharves, then usually crowded
with naval vessels or 'prizes' captured from the French.

His family was not poor, and so did not suffer from the
extortionate food prices which were a consequence of the war.

The Cornish miners and their families, hit by the decline in
the overseas tin market, however, were desperate, and they took
their own measures against profiteers and hoarders of precious
grain, roaming in gangs to demolish the bakers' shops, corn mills,
and granaries of those they suspected.

Five hundred of them, armed with heavy clubs, invaded
Falmouth, just as a coaster loaded with grain arrived.

A Captain Kempthorne, overseeing the discharge of the cargo,
seeing the miners lining up in threatening array, acted quickly.
He placed six-year-old James on the topmost sack, and asked him
to sing a well known Methodist hymn.

Amused to hear the shrill solo, the miners, many of whom had
frequented Wesley's mass meetings, took up the hymn full
throatedly, and then dispersed quietly.

When barely 10, he went to sea as cabin boy on the Government
Packet 'Lady Harriet.' On a voyage to Lisbon she was captured

James Silk Buckingham

by the French and James, with the rest of the crew, put into prison at Corunna.

He was lucky. The gaoler's daughter (she was about his own age) took a real fancy to him and fed him well on dainties from her father's table.

In fact she offered to let him out—if he would elope with her! James was of a more practical turn of mind, and when (probably to get him out of the way) her father freed him and pointed him in the general direction of Lisbon, he tramped the three hundred miles, barefoot, and begging his food, and when there had the sense to seek out a British warship, the 'Prince of Wales', which took him home.

His widowed mother begged him to give up the sea, and when

he was old enough, set him up in a small stationer's shop in Falmouth.

When he was 18, his mother died and within the year he had married a local farmer's daughter. Restless, he tired of the shop, and went to Plymouth, and volunteered for the Navy. Within weeks he saw a fellow sailor flogged to within an inch of his life, and decided promptly the Navy was not for him, jumped into an empty boat at Saltash, and ran off home to Falmouth.

Probably he managed to buy himself out, for his next venture was a Devonport bookshop. When a relative of his wife embezzled some money, he found bankruptcy threatened, and perhaps saw it as an excuse to be off to sea again.

He sailed to Trinidad on the 'Titus' as Chief Officer. Precocious as ever, at 22, he was commander of his own vessel, and made several voyages to the Eastern Mediterranean.

He had a fantastic ability to pick up languages, and was soon competent in French, Italian, Greek, and, more important, Arabic. He was able, in Cairo, to gain the confidence of the 'Pasha', Mahomet Ali, and, sixty years before De Lesseps, and Disraeli, tried to sell him the idea of a canal across the Isthmus of Suez.

With political insight, the wily ruler told him: 'It would be like sharpening a knife for my own throat,' for England would not rest until she controlled it—and Egypt.

On an expedition up the Nile, Buckingham was attacked by mutinous troops, and left, in the desert, naked and without food or water. Somehow, he struggled back to the river and a boat to safety.

Undaunted, he dressed Lawrence-like as a Bedouin, and made a detailed chart of the Red Sea. The Pasha, much impressed, suggested he try to establish a trade route from India, via the Red Sea, as, even with transhipment, there would be great advantages over the very long route around the Cape.

In Bombay, Buckingham was regarded as a cheeky interloper, by the East India Company, which had a centuries old monopoly on trade with Europe.

When he sought to do business with the ruler of a native state, they banned him from every British controlled port. Back in

Egypt, he was encouraged to try again; this time, as Mahomet Ali's official representative, he could not be banned.

In Mohammedan dress, and with a flowing beard he went, via Palestine and modern Iraq, to the Persian Gulf, to set sail for Bombay. Still refused the East India Company's cooperation, he took service with the Sultan of Muscat, for some years captaining the magnificent 'Humayoon Shah,' trading in eastern and far eastern waters.

He threw up the post, which had earned him a fortune, when asked to sail to Zanzibar on a slaving trip, in 1818.

Next, he became the very prosperous editor-proprietor of the Calcutta Mirror. When the popular paper began to attack the East India Company's monopoly, and the widespread corruption it tolerated, it was suppressed.

Buckingham, having spent much of his fortune in legal battles with the Company, went back to Britain. After the 1832 Reform Bill, Buckingham was elected to Parliament, as M.P. for Sheffield.

Here he was well-placed to campaign against the East India Company's abuses. He also backed a bill to abolish flogging as a punishment in the services, long his aim.

A temperance enthusiast, he also presided over a committee which collected valuable evidence on the effects of alcohol abuse. In 1837, he went on a tour of the U.S.A. which lasted four years. His public sevices were rewarded in 1851 by the award of a 'Civil List' pension of £200 per annum. He died four years later, aged 70.

Three years later, the old enemy, the East India Company, was wound up following the Mutiny.

John Couch Adams, The Farmer's Son Who Found A Planet

John Couch Adams was born at Laneast, six miles from Launceston, on the edge of Bodmin Moor, in 1819. His father was a tenant farmer. He learnt to read and write, and most importantly the rudiments of arithmetic, at a 'dame school,' before going to work on the farm. He often tended the sheep on the downs, where, in the night hours, he spent much time literally 'star-gazing.' At home was a simple book on astronomy, which had belonged to a grandfather, and from it he began to comprehend something of the solar system. He made himself a sun dial, and a cardboard sextant.

His exceptionally understanding father saw that he was more suited to study than farm work, and sent him to a school in Devonport, run by a clergyman relative of his mother. In his spare time he read every book on astronomy in the local 'Mechanics Institute' library. He began to draw maps of the stars and to compute (long before computers existed) celestial phenomena, for his latent mathematical ability was immense. On first looking through a telescope at the moon, he exclaimed: 'Why they have Roughtor and Brown Willy up there!' These Cornish peaks were not much more than an hour's walk from his sheepfold. His account of a solar eclipse, observed by him at Devonport, 'through a small spyglass,' got printed in a London paper, and in 1839, when he was twenty he seized the only chance in his life time to see Halley's Comet, which he spotted after a three week watch. His proud father then found a method by which he could go to Cambridge University. This was as a 'poor sizar,'

John Couch Adams

which meant that in exchange for some menial duties there, he would be given virtually free tuition. He amply repaid the confidence of the local dignitaries who had recommended him. Entering St. John's College in 1839, he, in 1843, graduated as 'Senior Wrangler,' (the best mathematician of his session) and was subsequently elected a 'fellow' and appointed as a tutor of his college.

While still an undergraduate, he noticed an unexpected deviation in the expected course of the planet Uranus, and thought it must be due to the attraction of an (as yet) unsuspected planet. Joyfully accepting the challenge he began a 'space exploration on paper,' and worked out the position of the unknown body, as surely as if he were equipped with the technical hardware of the 20th century scientist. He at once sent the papers to the Astronomer Royal, who, giving little weight to the assertion of a 24 year old newcomer, locked them in his desk for future examination. He was anyway of the opinion that if the planet existed, it would not be seen until the beginning of the 21st century, after two revolutions of Uranus had been completed. Almost a year after Adams had submitted his work, the French mathematician, Leverrier, who had approached the problem from another angle, and by a more laborious method, had calculated where the planet should be, and immediately had his conclusion confirmed by the observation of a French astronomer. Though he was dis- appointed, Adams flew into no tantrum, but rather, happily compared notes with Leverrier, only observing that he wished English astronomers had taken the trouble to look and so got the credit for this country.

In 1846, the embarrassed Astronomer Royal laid Adams' paper before the Royal Astronomical Society, which confirmed his claim, and the scientific world split into those who recognised Adams, and the supporters of Leverrier. John Adams himself was uninterested in the controversy. He declined the knighthood offered in 1847, as he did the office of Astronomer Royal, when it fell vacant in 1881, quite happy in his academic career at Cambridge. This was consistent with the character of the man. A Cornish lady, Miss Caroline Fox, who, in 1847, met the newly famous Adams, when he dined with her at a gentleman's home, wrote that he was 'a quiet looking man, with a broad forehead, a mild face, and an amiable and expressive mouth.' Of his discovery she concluded: 'The delight of working it out was far more than any notoriety could give, for his love of pure truth is evidently intense, an inward necessity unaffected by all the penny trumpets of the world.' She added, 'he is a most good son and neighbour, and watchful in the performance of small acts of thoughtful kindness.' Sixteen years later she visited him at Cambridge, probably as much to be able to report back to Cornwall on the wife he had just married, a Dublin lady, Miss Eliza Bruce, as to observe his studies. She describes the mechanical calculating machine (invented by Cambridge Professor William French) which Adams used to speed his researches: 'It can multiply or divide ten figures accurately.' She observed that he enjoyed all things great and small with a boyish zest. Baring Gould, who also frequently met him there, wrote that he loved a joke, and would join heartily in games with his friends' children. Strange that, at this very time, another Cambridge mathematics lecturer, Charles Dodgson (alias Lewis Carroll) was writing 'Alice in Wonderland.' He was, Baring Gould tells us, not utterly absorbed in mathematics and astronomy, 'botony, geology, history, and divinity all had their share of his attention.'

It is a measure of his modesty, and his gratitude and loyalty to his father that, on one occasion, when he went back to Laneast, and he asked him to drive a flock of sheep into Launceston Market as he used to do, the newly fledged professor cheerfully obliged. Incidentally, he did not have the monopoly of brains in the family. His brother William, 17 years his junior, became Professor of Natural Philosophy, and of Astronomy, in King's College, London University. No doubt John's success and probably financial help, made the way easier for him.

Nevil Northey Burnard
Self taught master sculptor

Artistic genius (like Longfellow's arrow shot into the air) 'comes to earth one knows not where.'

In the eighteenth century, it was at Plympton where, when Grammar School Headmaster Samuel Reynolds showed a local dignitary a pencil sketch by his son Joshua, he sagely remarked that 'he who drew that would be the first hand in England.'

Eighty years later it was at the village of Altarnun, on Bodmin Moor, where a 16-year-old stonemason's son sculpted in slate so remarkable a piece of work that it was exhibited at a session of the 'Cornish Polytechnic Society', and awarded a silver medal.

The point is that the subject of both young artists was the same, a representation of the classical Greek sculpture 'Laocoon' showing a father and his two sons being strangled by huge serpents.

Reynolds must have first seen a picture of the sculpture in one of the many books available to him in the home of his father, or of Lord Mount Edgcumbe, which he often visited as a lad. Nevil Northey Burnard had copied it from a woodcut in the 'Penny Magazine'.

Reynolds received a good classical education from his father. Burnard's mother kept a 'Dame School', and it was from her that he acquired a literacy by no means to be dispised.

This busy lady added to the family finances by making straw hats in her spare time, but money was never that plentiful and at the time he started to work for his father as a mortar boy, the price of a proper stone chisel was beyond him.

However, he sharpened nails on a grindstone as a substitute

Nevil Northey Burnard

and, to produce a smooth surface on the 'Delabole' slate, he used a quarter section of an old millstone, which he set in a rough wooden frame, producing quite a professional finish.

His sculpting started when he asked to do the lettering on a baby cousin's tombstone. His father thinking the grass would soon cover any errors, let him do the bottom line, instead of incising the letters, he cut round them so that they stood out in relief.

He loved to carve the figures of men and animals and had a gift for portraits. He carved the head and shoulders of Wesley, above the Methodist Meeting House door at Trewint, when he was sixteen.

After his triumph at the Cornish Polytechnic Society exhibition, Sir Charles Lemon became his patron, and he was presented to Queen Victoria, and allowed to cut a portrait of the boy Prince of Wales. The copy, in marble, he made for the Public Hall, at Falmouth.

Royal patronage led to very well paid work, in the best London studios, where he, like Reynolds before him, met the great and the famous. Thomas Carlyle was one of those who encouraged him, and he exhibited at the Royal Academy, first in 1855, when he was 37, and three more times over a twenty year period. Little of the sophistication of the circle he moved in in London rubbed off on him, he was described as 'mixing with the highest, but, by preference with the lowest.'

A lady, who dined once with him, condescendingly wrote: 'He is a great powerful, pugilistic looking fellow . . . a great deal of face, with all the features massed in the centre; mouth open and all sorts of simplicities flowing out of it.'

Her description of his face is partly borne out by his self-portrait, a cameo in plaster of Paris, but she gravely underestimated his intellectual capacity. This verse, from a poem he wrote, to console the parents of a friend, who died unexpectedly, shows that:

> *I now can see what might have been my story,*
> *Had I remained through man's allotted day;*
> *(Sorry for joy, dark age for youth and glory:)*
> *And bless the love that hastened me away.*
> *And wafted me across the mystic river,*
> *Where all discords and elements agree,*
> *Calmed by His word, that can from death deliver,*
> *So tell my loved ones not to mourn for me.*

The Laocoön, executed at age 16

He was himself to experience many of the vicissitudes of which he wrote. He married a London girl, but she died, and sad and lonely, he took to drink, and went 'on tramp'.

He could always earn money, by drawing sketches, or portraits, for customers in the pubs he visited, or at farms he called in at, on the road.

He also wrote occasional articles for newspapers, and would (for a consideration) write a hard-hitting 'squib' for either side in an election.

He was an entertaining conversationalist, with plenty of recollections to draw on. He told of the time he was an assistant in the studio of a world famous sculptor.

When the great man died his widow came into the studio with a hammer, and knocked off the noses of several completed busts, 'so that they might not be too common!'

He often visited Altarnun, to look up old friends. It did not bother him that he slept in a cheap lodging house, and was given by them new clothes to replace those ragged from his travels.

Sketches surviving from his last year show that his artistic skill never diminished. He died, in Redruth Workhouse, of a kidney complaint, in November, 1878.

Trevithick
An unrewarded genius

The 'horseless carriage' was still a rarity on our roads at the beginning of the present century, but, a hundred years earlier, a Cornish genius had made one, and driven it three hundred miles to London. It was, of course, steam-powered, and as the first railway engine had yet to be constructed, Richard Trevithick, as the 'Yuri Gagarin' of the steam transport age, should have gained instant fame and swiftly following fortune. There was however a great obstacle, the private owners of the new 'turnpike' roads did not intend to let them be ruined by the heavy machine, and spoil the profitable coach trade.

Born at Illogan, near Redruth, in 1771, he was thirty when he achieved a permanent place in all future record books, and already had many notable engineering achievements to his credit. He had been famed for his physique and wrestling skill before be became known as an engineer. A well-built six feet two inches in height, he excelled at hammer throwing, and could raise from the ground a weight of half a ton. When, later in life he was attacked by two London 'muggers', he nonchalantly banged their heads together and sent them reeling in opposite directions, but although he could show temper, he was usually almost too easy going.

Quick to learn from his father, and other engineers, when only twenty, he was asked to select the best type of engine for the tin mine where he was employed. Soon he was to construct an engine which made even the famous James Watt's productions seem old-fashioned. Trevithick's 'High Pressure' engine could pump the same amount of water, using only half the coal. Watt's engines relied on condensation causing a partial vacuum to withdraw the piston after a steam powered stroke, Trevithick used steam pressure in both directions. There was great rivalry and jealousy, where fortunes were at stake, Watt said Trevithick's invention was a public danger, and he 'deserved hanging' for it. Trevithick's business sense was always abysmal, and, pressed for ready cash, he sold a half share in his patent for a mere £200.

It was on Christmas Day, 1801, that Trevithick amazed the people of Camborne by putting his first locomotive on the road. The 'Puffing Devil', as they christened it, was able to carry a dozen passengers uphill faster than they could walk. Its 'teething troubles,' are said to have originated the anthem of the 'well-oiled' Cornish Rugby player 'Going up Camborne hill coming down.' Soon however regular runs were made, as far as Plymouth. When, eventually, the vehicle got to London and stormed, puffing steam, at a marvellous twelve miles an hour, along Oxford Street, all horses and carriages were ordered away, and many shops closed for fear of accidents. Trevithick then exhibited his invention on a circular track. He was the first to put a smooth iron wheel on a smooth rail, achieving the low friction that made possible the whole future railway system. Others, such as his friend Stephenson, were to reap the reward. Trevithick was ahead of the demand, and when the engine wore out, and capital ran out, could get no further with this project. He had other irons (far too many) in the fire. There was the tunnel under the Thames, which he came within 100 feet of completing, when it flooded. Typically, he nearly drowned, as he insisted on seeing all of his workmen out. There was the screw propeller the Admiralty did not yet want, and, in 1813, be became engrossed in the Plymouth Breakwater project, the next year he invented the steam threshing machine, the start of mechanised farming.

In 1816, he was awarded what seemed a marvellous contract to construct pumping engines for Peru's silver mines. This he accomplished, to great acclaim, and was about to reap a rich reward, but alas this was South America, there was the inevitable revolution, and his engines were thrown down the mine shafts, by the enemies of his Peruvian partners. He was actually impressed into Bolivar's revolutionary army. Stopping only to invent for them a new carbine, with an explosive bullet, he took the first chance to slip away, and reach, after a series of 'Boys Own Paper' adventures, Costa Rica, where he opened up hitherto inaccessible silver mines. At one point he turned surgeon and carried out a successful double amputation on a miner trapped by the legs. He finally decided enough was enough when his boat capsized in a Colombian river, and he was lassoed and dragged ashore semi- conscious to the disappointment of a pursuing alligator. It is ironical that he had to borrow the passage money home from Robert Stephenson (George's son) then in Colombia on a construction project. He had last seen him when he held him on his knee as an infant.

Home with nothing but a gold watch, a compass, and pair of dividers to his name, Camborne church bells rang out and he was invited into all the local great houses, as a celebrity. When however he tried to raise funds from the mine-owners who had saved hundreds of thousands of pounds by using his inventions he was ignored.

Like Bruce's spider he tried again! He produced plans for an iron ship, a recoil gun carriage for the army, a plant to make ice using steam, a chain pump for draining the Dutch marshes. He made great improvements which halved the weight and size of marine engines and halved the fuel they consumed. He died on 22 April, 1833, at Dartford, when working on these engines. Penniless he was indebted to charity for his grave, the mechanics at the factory were his bearers and only mourners. It does somehow seem fitting that the last rites for this magnificent engineer were performed, out of respect, by fellow technicians.

A Magnificent Obsession

Samuel Plimsoll is a name for quiz-masters to conjure with. There is a distinctly more than even chance that a dim, or nervous contestant will gladly grasp the lifeline, when his name is mentioned, and correctly answer that it was his persistent efforts that resulted in a law enforcing the marking of a 'load line' on all merchant ships. It was this that checked the unnecessary loss of life on over-loaded, over-insured, and unseaworthy 'coffin ships.' This act was passed in 1876, but half a century before an obscure Cornish cabinet-maker had started a campaign which would save as many lives at sea, but who today remembers Henry Trengrouse?

He was born at Helston in 1772, a period when the dangerous coastline of the Cornish peninsula was not the only menace faced by the crews of sailing ships who might perish from the activities of deliberate 'wreckers', or having struggled ashore exhausted from an accidental shipwreck, suffer the fate of Admiral Sir Cloudesley Shovel, who had the rest of the life choked out of him on a Scilly beach, by those who stole the jewellery he was wearing. There were, of course, many other Cornishmen who risked their lives, as they still do, to rescue shipwrecked mariners, and Cornwall can always point to the work of Trengrouse as making amends. It was not however until he was thirty-five that he took any interest in this matter. In that year, 1807, in the week after Christmas, the navigator of H.M.S. Anson, on a dark and stormy night, mistook Land's End for The Lizard, which he thought he had rounded, and so was heading straight up channel for Plymouth. Instead the Anson sailed straight onto the Loe Bar, a sand and pebble ridge, some three miles from Helston.

Many of those on board scrambled ashore, along a broken mast, but, though it seemed as if all might have left the ship, two Methodist local preachers, Messrs. Roberts and Foxwell, risked their lives to see if any were left. When they got on board they found two women and two children, and several men. They managed to save the women and some men, but the children were drowned in the attempt. As was the custom then, the many bodies washed ashore were bundled into large pits near the shore and interred without any burial ceremony, or careful identification. The exact number who died was unknown, as it is believed that some of the press-ganged crew, and soldiers on board, took a golden opportunity to desert! Henry Trengrouse was among those who watched the tragedy from the shore, and from that day became utterly determined to find ways of preventing such loss of life. Every spare penny he had was devoted to life-saving experiments. He did a great deal of work on improving lifeboats, and the cork lined life-saving jacket was his idea, but his best inspiration came to him while watching, on Helston Green, the King's birthday celebrations. He saw rockets blazing their arcs through the sky and wondered if instead of trailing sparks, they might trail a thin line, which could thus be fired across a stormy sea, and then used to pull across a cable from ship to shore, along which by pulleys a crew could travel to safety.

A Captain Manby had earlier had a similar idea, but this involved using a heavy mortar to fire a barbed shot, attached to a line. There were several snags, first, rapid acceleration on firing often broke the line, also the apparatus was very heavy and took a long time to drag to the cliff, or other firing site. There was also danger to people on board the distressed vessel, and after several had been killed in experiments the idea was abandoned. A rocket, Trengrouse saw, would accelerate gradually, so reducing the chances of a line snapping, also the apparatus could be very light and easily transported to a vantage point. He also saw the obvious advantage in ships carrying rockets, as a coastline was a vast target, while a ship bobbing on a wild sea was much more difficult to hit.

Once he had perfected the invention, his most difficult and expensive task was ahead of him. Niggardly shipowners were likely to think him an interfering crank, as was their attitude later to Plimsoll, an Act of Parliament would be necessary to make sure that all vessels carried the rocket apparatus. And the Admiralty had to be persuaded to set up stations along the coast. To lobby Parliament, he many times made the four day coach journey to London, even in winter, which undermined his health. He had already expended £3,000, and was practically penniless, when he got a legacy of £500, and that went as well.

At last, the Admiralty decided to take twenty of his rockets, and then decided they would make them in their own yards. They awarded Trengrouse just £50, to cover lost profit! This, and a £30 prize from the Society of Arts, was all he ever received. Foreign powers were more appreciative, the Russian ambassador offered him every support and facility to make his rockets in Petrograd. 'My own country first,' was Trengrouse's answer. The Czar still showed his appreciation by giving him a diamond ring, but this he was forced to pawn, and could never redeem. The pity is that Trengrouse, quite as dedicated as Plimsoll was, did not have the wealth derived from a successful business career behind him, nor the 'clout' of the influential M.P. that Plimsoll was. It was only in 1907, when he had been dead fifty years, that the Dutch government became the first to order rockets to be carried on all sizeable ships. For many years before that however his apparatus had been saving lives. Official Board of Trade figures show that, between 1870 and 1907, 8,924 people owed their lives to his invention.

When, at 82, he lay dying, his last words, spoken to his son, were, 'If you live to be as old as I am, you will find my rocket apparatus all along our shores.' There is no doubt that, since the day he had seen the bodies from the wreck of the Anson lying on the beach, he had been obsessed with the idea of saving lives from shipwrecks, but what a magnificent obsession!

When the Fairies went to Bodmin Gaol

Leprechauns in Ireland, and pixies in Cornwall, now seem to be only of the variety found on the shelves of the tourists shops, but I well remember older Cornish women, when bothered by the inexplicable disappearance of some article, or otherwise flustered, exclaiming 'I must be piskie-laden.' Certainly, in 17th century Cornwall, most people really believed in the existence of the 'little people.'

In 1696, Moses Pitt, a publisher, who had spent most of his working life in London, wrote a letter to the Bishop of Gloucester, containing a long account of strange happenings, remembered from his boyhood, on the family farm at St. Teath, eight miles north of Bodmin. The family had, as was the custom, taken into the household a poor girl, a parish apprentice, to work in return for food and clothing, until the age of 21. In far too many cases this could mean virtual slavery, but the Pitts tended to spoil young Anne Jefferies, described as 'a girl of a bold, daring spirit, who would venture at those difficulties and dangers that no boy would attempt.'

In 1645, when she was about 19, she had a sudden nervous and physical breakdown. There were frequent fits, 'into which she would fall if vexed,' and she became too weak to walk, without clinging to some support. Moses wrote that she became 'even as a changeling,' to him the word meant replaced in spirit by an elf or fairy. However, as she grew stronger, she delighted to go to the church, to hear the preacher read the gospel (she could not herself read at all.) She still remained too 'silly,' to be left alone in the house. This presented a problem to the good farmer's wife, when one day, with everyone else in the harvest field, she discovered she was out of flour with which to cook the evening meal. Corn had been sent to the mill, a quarter of a mile away, but the miller had not, as promised, brought the flour. She could not send Anne, and went herself, first persuading the rather reluctant young woman, to wait in the garden, and locking the door, to avoid her accidentally setting fire to the house. On the way back from the mill, Mrs. Pitt fell and badly hurt her leg. A passing neighbour brought her home on his horse, and the alarmed harvesters all ran back to the house. So painful was the leg, that a servant was told to saddle up a horse and ride to Bodmin to fetch Surgeon Lobb. Then Anne came forward and told her mistress how sorry she was that she had fallen, incidentally mentioning the exact place the accident occurred. She asked repeatedly to see the leg, and, to humour her, Mrs. Pitt consented. As she stroked it, the pain rapidly grew less intense. Anne begged her not to send for the surgeon, as she herself would 'by the blessing of God,' cure her leg. The man was told not to go, and very soon the leg was completely healed.

Her mistress then realised that Ann had, before she had been allowed to see her leg, mentioned the exact place that the mishap had occurred. Curious, she asked her how she knew this, as only the man who brought her home could have told her, and he had departed before Anne came on the scene. She replied that half a dozen people had told her, and when Mrs. Pitt pointed out that this was not possible, she was told this remarkable tale. Anne said that the reason for her sudden illness was what happened on a day that she was knitting stockings, 'in an arbour of the garden,' and over the hedge there came suddenly: 'six small people all in green clothes, which put me into such a fright, that was the start of my sickness, and they continue their appearance to me. They always come in even numbers, 2, 4, 6, or 8. When I said often in my illness, they had just gone out of the window . . . you thought me light-headed. Today when you put me out into the garden, they came to me, and I told them that I was unwilling to come out of the house. They said you should not fare better for it, and, at that time, in a fair pathway, you fell and hurt your leg.'

The story of Anne's ability to cure spread rapidly, she had visitors from all over Cornwall, even from London, 'to seek cures for all distempers, sicknesses, and sores.' Although she was never observed to take any money, she handed out salves and medicines, without buying any from apothecaries, and was never seen making them. Even more strange, Moses relates: 'She forsook eating our victuals and was fed by those fairies from the harvest time to the next Christmas Day, when, because it was that day, she said she would eat some roast beef with us at our table.' On one occasion, he wrote: 'I looked through the keyhole of the door of her chamber, and saw her eating; and when she had done eating, she stood still by the bedside as long as thanks might be given, and then she made a curtesy (or bend) and opened the chamber door, and gave me a piece of the bread, which I did eat, and I think it was the most delicious bread that ever I did eat, either before or since.'

Another inexplicable thing was that Anne 'would tell what people would come to her, several days before they came, and from whence, and at what time.' Moses said he often saw Anne in the garden dancing, she said with the fairies, although he could not see them. However a four year old sister said she had seen them, and more surprisingly their mother, Mrs. Pitts had said she saw them once, and heard them talking about taking food to Anne.

Anne's reputation attracted the attention of ministers and magistrates, who closely examined her, and she seemed to have rational answers. The ministers told her the fairies were evil spirits, sent from the devil. When they were gone, Anne said the fairies were calling her to her room, and could not be dissuaded from going there. Later, she returned with a Bible, turned to a verse in the Epistle of St. John: 'Beloved, believe not every spirit, but try the spirits whether they be of God.' As Anne could not read, the family assumed the fairies had found the page for her. One day, when Anne was milking a cow, the fairies appeared, to tell her a constable was coming to take her to Bodmin Gaol, but that she was not to resist, as all would be well. The prison warders were strictly under orders to give her no food, yet she lived there for weeks without complaint or loss of weight, fed, the Pitt family firmly believed, by the fairies. When the sessions came Moses Pitt's mother, and then he himself, were summoned as witnesses.

They were first searched to see that they were carrying her no food. No sentence was passed on Anne, who remained in gaol some weeks longer, and was then discharged into the custody of the magistrate who brought the original charge. At his house also she was given no food, but continued healthy. Not allowed to return to the farm at St. Teath, she went to stay at Padstow, with Farmer Pitt's widowed sister, and there too she continued with her cures. Eventually she married, William Warren, a farm hand, and went to live in Devon.

Moses Pitt informed the Bishop that he had tried to get the still living Anne to give him her account of the events of fifty years previous, but she had blankly refused to cooperate. She said he would only 'make books or ballads of it, and she would not have her name spread about the country in such things, if she might have £500 for doing so.' Even if her father were still alive, she would not tell him anything. She had been questioned by magistrates and judges, and believed if she started talking about such things now, the same thing would happen. The old lady was very wise, and probably was well aware that in the social climate of the time she was lucky not to have already been drowned, or burned, as a witch.

The Rev. Baring Gould summed up the story thus: 'The cures she wrought are to be put into the category of faith cures the world over, whether performed at Lourdes, or by Christian Scientists, or by Shamans in the Steppes of Tartary.' He does admit that her ability to go so long without normal food, even while under observation in prison, is harder to account for.

They Hung At Bodmin

On the morning of February 8, 1840, Mr Nevill Norway, a thirty-nine-year old Wadebridge timber merchant, mounted his grey horse, and rode the nine miles to Bodmin, for the market, where he would be meeting clients and creditors, in the course of his business.

At 4 pm, he had occasion to take out of his purse some gold and silver coins to settle a debt. Watching him at the time was one of his neighbours.

If he had not recognised the neighbour, he would have recognised the coat he was wearing, one of his own old garments he had charitably given him a few days previously.

This neighbour, William Lightfoot, and his younger brother James, both in their thirties, stayed on in Bodmin after the market closed, probably patronising the busy taverns.

They did not leave until late in the evening, and were glimpsed by a shoemaker making his way home, in the grounds of a deserted cottage, on the Wadebridge road.

Riderless hope

Mr Norway had remained with friends in Bodmin until 10 pm, when he, too, rode off with a companion on the road home. His companion branched off, after three miles, and he rode on alone.

A farmer, also bound for Wadebridge, saw a grey horse just ahead, saddled and bridled, but riderless. It galloped off as he

Old Bodmin Gaol

approached. Some pedestrians who had seen it go by, told the farmer it was Mr Norway's horse.

He therefore went to Mr Norway's house, and found the horse standing outside the stable. There was blood on the saddle. Two of Mr Norway's servants, having called out the local surgeon, set out with lanterns to look for their master, but it was daybreak before they saw him.

He was lying on his back, in a small stream, and quite dead. The surgeon examined the body and found injuries about the face and head, obviously from some blunt instrument.

A pool of blood was found in the nearby road, and tracks in the intervening field indicated that the corpse had been dragged to the stream by more than one man.

The field was opposite the house in which the Lightfoots had been lurking. Close to the blood on the road, was found the snapped off hammer of a pistol. Mr Norway's purse and his keys were missing.

There was no direct evidence to lead at once to the murderers, but a detective constable called Jackson came down from London and soon suspected the Lightfoots.

He found a pistol, without one of its hammers, concealed in the beams of James Lightfoot's house, and took him to Bodmin for questioning.

The shaken William blurted out to a crony that he was 'in it as well as James.' The news got quickly to Constable Jackson, who arrested him.

He at once made a statement, admitting that he had been with James and had seen him murder Mr Norway. In fact, on the way to Bodmin jail, he pointed out the gorse bush where that gentleman's keys had been flung, and they were recovered.

When William arrived at the jail, James, in turn, named him as the actual murderer. On March 30, both were found guilty and sentenced to hang. They 'received the sentences with great stolidity.' They were now put in the same cell, and immediately flew at each other's throats, and had to be separated while awaiting execution.

On Monday, April 13, 1840, they were hanged before a huge crowd.

The report in the West Briton said: 'Bodmin on Sunday evening presented the appearance of a fair. There were two shows (one, a 'Feast of Horrors') stationed in the High Street, ready for the next day. Every public house, as well as private houses, was filled to overflowing. Thousands of people traversed the high roads during the night.

'On Monday morning the public houses were teeming with multitudes, and the demand was so great, in those frequented by the poorer classes, that beer sold at 9d a quart.

'A large open space, below the drop, was occupied by the sheriff's javelin men (the judge's escort) and the local and special constables. In the fields beyond, persons started to assemble at dawn, and by noon, the hour of execution, there could not have been less than twenty thousand.

'They were both launched into eternity at once. They died almost immediately. The shoe of William, through the jerk, fell off. After hanging for an hour, the bodies were cut down, and put into a couple of black coffins, with the ropes around their necks. They were then buried in a hole, about three feet deep, in the coal yard, just in front of the prison.'

All the sympathy of Cornish people was saved for Mr Norway's fatherless family, and £3,500 was collected for them.

There is an extraordinary supernatural twist to this story. Mr Norway's brother, Edmund, was at the time of his murder, the Captain of a merchantman, and in the South Atlantic. In his ship's log, the morning after the tragedy, he recorded a vivid dream he had during the night of February 8.

It contained all the details of the scene, even including the use of the pistol, as a bludgeon, when it had twice misfired, and the discovery of the body in the stream. On awaking, he consoled himself with the thought that one thing in the dream was certainly wrong, and so perhaps the rest could be.

Cottage error

He recollected that the cottage in which the murderers concealed themselves appeared on the left hand side of the road, and having actually passed it many times, knew it was on the right.

What he did not know was that, in the long period he had been at sea, the road has been realigned to pass the cottage on the other side!

This is either a most remarkable example of telepathy, or (in view of the fact that the logbook does not appear to have been preserved) one of those stories, much improved in the telling, called by cynical Devonian neighbours of the Cornish, 'Cousin Jack Stories.'

More Things In Heaven And Earth

Millions vividly remember seeing President Kennedy assassinated, only scores saw the killing of President Lincoln. Such are the dubious benefits of television, radio, or for that matter undersea cable, that news of such sensational crimes is now received almost instantaneously around the world. It is strange to reflect that it was nearly three weeks before Lincoln's assassination, in 1865, was heard of in Europe. More than fifty years before this, in the lobby of the House of Commons, on the evening of May 12th, 1812, occurred the one and only assassination of a British Prime Minister, that of Spencer Perceval who was simultaneously the Chancellor of the Exchequer. Given the speed of the fastest post-horse, it would have been the morning of the 12th May before the people of, say Bristol, would have heard the shocking news. Yet, before midnight on the 11th, more than twice the distance from London, at Scorrier on the outskirts of Truro, a fully detailed account of the event was being given.

John Williams of Scorrier was at this time the 'most extensive mining adventurer in Cornwall.' This hard-headed engineer and business man, had, on May 11th, gone to bed at his customary time and soon fell asleep, but quickly awoke from a most vivid dream. He told his wife that he had dreamt he was in the lobby of the House of Commons, and 'saw a small man enter, dressed in a blue coat and a white waistcoat. Immediately after he saw a man dressed in a brown coat with yellow basket buttons draw a pistol from under his coat and discharge it at the former, who instantly fell, the blood issuing from a wound a little below the left breast. He heard the report of the pistol, saw the blood fly out and stain the waistcoat, and saw the colour of the face change.

He saw the murderer seized by some gentlemen who were present, and observed his countenance, and in asking who the gentleman was who had been shot, he was told it was the Chancellor.' Mrs. Williams naturally made light of the dream and advised her husband to forget it and go to sleep. This he did, but soon woke to say he had dreamed exactly the same thing again. He was so agitated when he, after dropping off again, had this 'vision' for the third time that, although it was only half past one in the morning, he got up and dressed and did not go back to bed.

At breakfast he was still full of the dream, and during the day, which he spent in Falmouth, he told any of his business acquaintances who would listen about it, obviously none of them had yet heard of the actual event. On the evening of the next day, the 13th May, his daughter, and son-in-law, Mr. Tucker, who had spent the day travelling down from their home at Trematon Castle, near Saltash, arrived at Scorrier. The still excited Mr. Williams did not give them time to sit down before he was relating the strange tale. His son-in-law, taking it that he referred to the *Lord* Chancellor, laughed and said that only in a dream would he be in the House of Commons, as he was a peer, but on hearing Mr. Williams' description said it indeed fitted the Chancellor of the Exchequer, Mr. Perceval. He quipped that although he had been his greatest enemy (Perceval had introduced some very unpopular taxes) he would not wish assassination on him! When Mr. Tucker enquired if his father-in-law had ever seen Mr. Perceval, he replied 'never,' and added that he had never visited the House of Commons either.

Almost immediately they heard a horseman gallop up to the door, and a son of Mr. Williams came rushing in to tell them that he had just come from Truro, where the latest arrivals on the London coach had brought news that the Prime Minister had indeed been killed. Six weeks later, Mr. Williams being in London on business, went to the spot where it had happened. Without being told, he pointed out where Bellingham, the assassin, stood when firing the shot, and exclaimed 'this place is as distinctly within my recollection in my dream as any in my house.' The whole story was sworn to by Mr. Williams in an affadavit witnessed by two local gentlemen, the Rev. Thomas

Fisher and Mr. Charles Prideaux Brune. The question is, what are we to make of it?

Let us assume the worst of Mr. Williams, could the whole thing have been 'set up', and more importantly, why? Certainly not to gain the reputation of a clairvoyant prophet, for he was hours late with the news. By what imaginable means could he have heard, directly, or indirectly of the event? Even a pigeon could not have made the journey quickly enough, and anyhow who would have despatched it to Truro. There was of course the possibility of visual telegraphy. This was the danger period of the Napoleonic war and the military had set up signalling stations to warn of invasion, such names as 'Telegraph Hill' still remind us of it, and the May evening might have afforded enough light to make this feasible. However, the message could not conceivably have been so detailed as the dream, and why should it have been communicated to a comparatively unknown Cornish mine proprietor, and to no one else in the area. If we examine the possibility that Mr. Williams had a much vaguer dream, which he later embroidered from newspaper reports, we have to forget the number of people to whom he mentioned the words 'Chancellor' and 'House of Commons', long before the official news reached Cornwall, or conclude that there was almost impossible collusion in deception by his family and acquaintances. The only near reasonable explanation we are left with is a kind of curiously delayed telepathy. The last word, I feel, is definitely with Shakespeare. There are indeed 'more things in Heaven and Earth than this world dreams of.'

Dead But He Wouldn't Lie Down

A few miles north of Saltash, on the Cornish side of the Tamar, is Pentillie Castle. It is not of any particular historical significance, but in the grounds, on a hill above the Tamar, with the Biblical name of 'Ararat,' is a red brick tower. The doorway has long been bricked up, but through two window slits can be seen, under the open sky, the statue of a seated man, life size, in early 18th century dress. An inscription reads:

> 'This Monument is erected in Memory of
> Sir James Tillie Knt. who dyed 15 of Novr.
> Anno Domini 1713, And in ye 67th. year of his Age.'

Among the startling traditions regarding this gentleman is the tale that he 'sold his soul to the devil,' but it is a lurid enough story, without such additions.

James Tillie was born in 1645, the son of a St. Keverne labourer, who placed him as 'servant of horseman to Sir John Coryton, of West Newton Ferrers, in the parish of St. Mellion.' The old Cornish historian Hals wrote: 'Afterwards, he, by his master's assistance learning the inferiour practice of the Lawe under an Atturney, became his Steward, in which caracter by his Care and Industry, he soon grew Rich, soe that he marryed Sir Henry Vane's daughter, by whome he had a good fortune, but noe issue.'

Why Sir John Coryton turned his coachman into a lawyer, we do not know, he might have had some unexplained hold over his master, but there is a possible reason that he was able to marry so well. Sir Henry Vane one of Cromwell's most important

Sir James Tillie

supporters, was, in 1662, executed for treason, on the return of the King, and few families would, at that time, have welcomed so politically compromised a bride. When Sir John died, in 1680, the 35 year old Tillie became 'Guardian in Trust for his younger children.' He also carried on as steward for the next Sir John Coryton, the older son, who had inherited the estates and title, and then married a wealthy heiress, Elizabeth Chiverton, daughter of a Lord Mayor of London. It was not long before he too died (the rumour was by poison.) Lady Elizabeth was far from inconsolable, and soon married the man with whom people said she had been over friendly, the 'upwardly mobile' steward, James Tillie, by then conveniently a widower. It is possible that jealousy at his meteoric rise led to rumours, not entirely dismissed by Hals, that he had an even more direct way of wealth creation than marrying heiresses, and that he was mixed up in the coining business: 'his steward Mr. Elliott, being credited for a mint and coyning false money for his use.' A later writer however concluded: 'If he got rich by nefarious practices, it was probably by filling his pockets out of the Coryton Estates, of which he was steward.'

However ill-gotten, his fortune was vast, and he used it first: 'to buy a great sume of money, and false reperesentation of himselfe,' obtain a knighthood from James II, and then to build Pentillie Castle. As time went, on and he still had no son to succeed him, he decided to leave his estate to his sister's son James Woolley, on condition that he changed his name to Tillie, and obeyed the instructions in a complicated will, one by which he hoped to dominate the family, long after his death. First he made ample provision for Lady Elizabeth (my dearest wife) to whom he left not only 'all her Paraphaanalia (sic), apparell, jewells and ornaments of her Person, all the Books, China, Portraits, and Toyes in her Closett at Pentillie Castle,' but, as well 'My Coach, Chariott, and set of six horses, with two such of my other horses and cowes as shall please her to elect, and also a Hundred Guineas in money for her life, and then for her grandchildren. To Altamira Tilley (presumably a daughter) he left £500, payable on the day she married either of his sister's sons, the sum to be halved, if she married anyone else. To 'my Cousin Mary Mattock £50, to be paid on her marriage Day with any other than William Parkes.' He shows more generosity in the treatment of his servants. To Richard Lawrence went 'meate and drink to the value of two shillings and sixpence per weeke during his life.' To all his domestic servants he left forty shillings, to Samuel Holman 'his Tooles,' and to John Long' a joynt of mutton weekly during his life, as I have done.'

Sir James Tillie's Monument at Pentillie

A quite bizarre section of the will dealt with the disposal of his body. According to Hals: 'He charged his heir that he should not inter his body in earth . . . but fasten it in the chair where he died with wire . . . his hat rings and best apparel on . . . and surround same with an oak chest, in which his books and papers should be laid, without Christian burial; for that as he said but an hour before he died, in two years space he would be at Pentillie again.' He was to build for the reception of the chest, a 'walled vault or grot, over this vault . . . a fine chamber, and set up thereon a picture of him, his lady, and adopted heir . . . whose successors are obliged to repair the same for ever, out of his lands and rents, on penalty of losing both.' The bill for the erection of the grandiose structure still exists. Of the outcome, Hals also wrote that four years later he heard: 'Sir James body is eaten out with worms, and his bones fallen to the ground.' The upper chamber has long collapsed, and there is no public access to what now remains of what was, in different senses, a monumental 'folly,' but, at least locally, the legend of the labourer's son, who made himself 'king' of his own castle lives on. Although the bones were removed by a later member of the family to St. Mellion Churchyard, they were replaced by the statue, perpetuating the spirit of his will.

Angry, Hungry Forties

When Napoleon's blockade prevented the importing of corn, though every cultivable acre came under the plough, grain reached famine prices. Housewives rioted in Plymouth, and in Cornwall mobs of miners confronted bakers and corn dealers with a hempen noose, as a strong hint that it would be prudent to moderate their charges. Many farmers thrived, and the rents they paid to their landlords increased sharply.

In 1815, when peace, and the prospect of imported wheat came, those landlords who had a clear majority in both Houses of Parliament sought to stave off a drop in their incomes by the Corn Laws. Imports of wheat were forbidden, until the price of home produced grain reached an exorbitant 80 shillings per quarter.

By the 1830's even the very labourers who harvested the grain were near starvation, and riots and rick burning had to be put down with a heavy hand.

In 1838, Quaker John Bright and Manchester merchant Richard Cobden started the Anti-Corn Law League. In 1843, Bright addressed an enthusiastic meeting of dockyardsmen in Devonport. The magistrates, fearing violence, ordered the police to 'distribute a sufficient force in the midst of the crowd.'

The watch Committee wisely saw that this would be provocation, and ordered the police merely to stand in readiness. This tactic paid off. There was a good deal of noise, but little disorder.

In 1846, the Corn Laws were repealed, but there was, at first, little effect on corn prices and 'Black 1847' was the worst year of all.

This was particularly so in Ireland, where blight destroyed the potato crop upon which the peasants depended. Soon there were many deaths from starvation, and a consequent intense hatred of absentee English landlords, carried across the Atlantic by thousands of desperate emigrants.

There was sympathy among ordinary folk in Britain. For example, in Camborne, a meeting was convened by the Vicar and the Methodist Minister to raise funds to help the Irish, and 'some handsome donations were announced.' However, there were those who complained that charity would be appropriate much nearer home.

The miners around Camborne and Redruth were themselves nearly starving, as the discovery of alluvial tin in Malaya, cheaply recovered by coolie labour, had closed down the Cornish mines as the market slumped.

The pages of the anti-Government West Briton are full of pathetic stories. One is of the Redruth landlord, who calling for overdue rent at dinnertime, found the family in his cottage 'frying turnips, with a little salt only'.

Many other families, the report continued, were subsisting on turnips, fried with the tallow of miners' candles.

'I was informed that a family of 11 persons had scarcely any other food for several days than at dinnertime, when they boiled the baking kettle, filled with water, which they thickened with a little barley meal, to which they added salt and sliced turnip.'

It is small wonder that in May, 1847, there were food riots in Wadebridge, where corn was being shipped out.

'Early on Thursday morning the owners of the corn in the cellars proceeded to ship it on a vessel when informed that a large body of men from Delabole quarries was approaching. Soon 400 men entered the town, and went at once to the Quay.

'It appearing that no outrage was likely, and that the men were really in want of food, the magistrates and others purchased all the bread in the town and distributed it amongst them.'

Just as they were leaving the town another large and much more threatening party of men arrived.

'They were (tin) streamers, china clay men, and tinners from Roche, Luxulyan, and St Austell. Armed with bludgeons, they marched to the Quay, cheering as they went.'

The vessel had by then cast off, and was moving down the

river. Despite the objections of the coast guards, the men insisted on the cellars being unlocked so that they could inspect them. When little corn was found, they left without causing any more trouble.

Three desperate miners of Lostwithiel—Semmens, Hambly, and Hencock—apparently helped themselves to a ram, belonging to a local farmer. In court, the police said they had found a neck of mutton boiling in Semmens' house, and some mutton suet.

Near the miners' workplace, they said they found a buried sack 'containing one fore and hind quarters of the ram.' A butcher witness made the rather suspect statement that he had matched the head and skin left in the field with these portions.

Only Semmens was at court. The other two had wisely 'fled the country.' He got 15 years transportation. A decade earlier, he would have hanged outside Bodmin goal.

A report of a meeting of the governors of that institution, in October 1847, illustrates the degree of general hunger: 'It was decided that vagrants should not be committed for more than 14 days, as they then had only bread and water. If in for a longer period, they were put on the full prison diet, which was so good they were not unwilling to come there again.'

Another report on Bodmin Assizes, gives us the story of young Richard James of Perranzabuloe.

He was walking along a road carrying 'two pasties, and two currant obbins' the dinners of four workmen his mother had prepared when, it was alleged, the prisoner Nathaniel Lanyon approached him, said 'he was starving and would have them,' then took all the dinners and walked away.

The boy went home and told his father and they gave a description to Truro police, who a month later arrested Lanyon. We do not read what the sentence was, but doubtless he stayed in Bodmin Gaol long enough to qualify for the full diet!

A poignant postcript is provided by official statistics, which show that in 1841, the average age of death in Liskeard was 43, in Bodmin 37, Truro 33, St Austell 32, and Camelford an awful 24.

Many miners died early of lung disease, but the level of infant mortality to produce these averages can be imagined.

Dolly Pentreath
Last Native Cornish Speaker

Visitors to Cornwall, almost as soon as they cross the Tamar, have around them, in just the names of towns and villages, incontrovertible evidence that they are in another country, rather than another county. Even the names of saints are not to be found anywhere else in Britain. While they stick to the popular resorts the language they hear around them will be English in all its varieties, even the shopkeepers tend to come from Brixton, or Birmingham, but the fishermen and the countryfolk, usually Cornishmen born and bred, like the Welsh and the Scots, speak English with an accent that has in it the echo of a native tongue. Even the grammatical construction of a sentence is different, again reflecting that of a language which dropped out of general use two centuries ago.

The last person reputed to have used it from birth was Dolly Pentreath, daughter of a Mousehole fisherman, who did not speak English until a grown woman. It is difficult to make a national heroine of someone whose only other recorded distinction was the ability to swear in English, or curse in Cornish with equal facility, and whose pleasure it was to swap dirty stories with cronies. She had the traditional vocabulary of the fishwife she was. As to being any other sort of wife, the records are not at all clear. She was born, and died, under the name of Pentreath, but there is a suggestion that, perhaps briefly, she was married to a man called Jeffry. This is possible, for young widows, unhappily, are often found in fishing villages. There is too, some evidence that she had an illegitimate child.

DOROTHY PENTREATH of MOUSEHOLE in CORNWALL.
the last Person who could converse in the Cornish Language?

Dolly Pentreath

She died in 1777, but her age then is a matter of dispute. Baptismal records can be confusing, and this was long before birth certificates, but she was said to have been 102. There is little doubt that she was selling fish in the villages around Mousehole, until she was well over 90. As a 'back-jouster,' she carried the fish in large baskets, as she walked from the harbour to her customers in the country houses and cottages, so must still have been quite strong. The claim that she was the last real Cornish speaker is strengthened by the fact that she was a legend in her own lifetime, even having her portrait painted. The origin of the illustration above is, that it is an etching after an oil painting at St. Michael's Mount. This was painted by fifteen year old John

Opie, the son of a mine carpenter, who afterwards became an R.A.

That Dolly was as wily as she was tough, is illustrated by the story of how she rescued a deserter from a 'man-of-war,' (probably a Cornish fisherman, who had been grabbed by the press gang) who ran into her house, with a posse of soldiers following a minute or so behind him. Quick witted Dolly sent

Opie's portrait of Dolly Pentreath

him up the chimney, where there was a cavity, which had probably been used for smuggled goods. She then threw on some furze to revive the fire, and put a crock filled with water over it. Drawing a wash tub to the hearth, she pulled up her skirts and sat with her feet in it, as if waiting for the water to heat. When an officer and his men burst in, she said that she was about to wash her feet, and swearing at them for molesting her, shouted in Cornish and English to the villagers to come to her aid. After a quick look around, the officer withdrew his men. Later the deserter, singed but safe, slipped away under the cover of darkness by sea to Guernsey.

Dolly's known relatives were living in Mousehole until the late 19th century, and those who know the little port might be interested as to where she lived. The tradition is that she first lived in a small court (long demolished) at the middle point of the harbour, later she moved to the house opposite the 'Keigwin Arms,' in which she died. Thousands have visited her memorial in nearby Paul Churchyard. It states that she was: 'said to have been the last person who conversed in the ancient Cornish, the peculiar language of this county, from the earliest records, until it expired, in the eighteenth century, in the parish of Paul.'

It is remarkable that the memorial, placed there as late as 1860, was paid for by a man, who though English by birth, was a nephew of Napoleon. Lucien Bonaparte was a linguistic expert, probably interested in Cornish as being so closely allied to the Breton tongue. It is pretty certain that Dolly would have been able to make herself understood by any Breton fishermen who sought shelter in Mousehole, in her day.

Mary's Marathon

Dick Whittington did it, although he almost gave up on the way, and others since, who also could afford no other form of transport, have walked to London from various parts of the Kingdom. Most of them had youth and ambition on their side. Mary Kelynack certainly lacked youth, for she was 84 years old when, in the late summer of 1851, she set out from Newlyn. She did have one great ambition. News had reached Cornwall of the Great Exhibition, which Queen Victoria and Prince Albert had opened in Hyde Park, and of the huge 'Crystal Palace,' which housed so many of the wonders of Britain and the Empire. The new railway network, which now had even reached as far west as Plymouth, was carrying people in their thousands from all parts of Britain to visit an exhibition which became such a success, that its profits provided future generations with such treasures as the Kensington Science Museum, and the Victoria and Albert Museum, and the Albert Hall, commemorating the Prince who masterminded the whole project. Mary, listening to the excited talk, and seeing those who could afford it setting off for the railway station at Plymouth, exclaimed, 'I'll go and see'n too I reckon!'

With a few shillings in her purse, she set off. This would have been madness for the more delicately nurtured, but the tough old fish-wife was a 'back-jouster', used to carrying her load of fresh fish along miles of country lanes to her customers. At a steady ten miles every weekday, she reached the capital in five weeks. She had sworn, before leaving she would accept no physical assistance, but did not object to financial contributions. No doubt the brave old lady was helped on her way by generous souls.

Mary Kelynack

On every great occasion the press look for 'human interest' stories, and Mary's fame had gone before her, the 'Illustrated London News,' related that 'On Tuesday September, 24th, among the visitors to the Mansion House was Mary Callinack, eighty-four years of age, who had travelled on foot from Penzance, carrying a basket on her head, with the object of visiting the Exhibition and of paying her respects personally to the Lord Mayor and Lady Mayoress. The Lord Mayor addressing her said: 'Well, I understand Mrs. Callinack, you have come to see me?'

She replied 'Yes, God bless you, I never was in such a place as this. I have come up asking for a small sum of money, I am sir.'

Mary told the Mayor that she had come from Penzance, and when he asked what had induced her to come to London, she said, 'I had a little matter to attend to, as well as to see the Exhibition. I was there yesterday, and I mean to go again tomorrow.' She had lodgings in Crawford St., Marylebone, just a mile away from the Exhibition, so this only involved a stroll across the park for the redoubtable octogenarian. The Mayor asked her what she thought of the Exhibition, and Mary said that it was very good, but that she had now spent all her money but 5½d. He chatted with her for some time, amused by her quaint conversation, and then gave her a sovereign, advising her to look out for thieves, who were everywhere among such crowds. Mary burst into tears of relief, saying, 'Now I will be able to get back.' She continued to get V.I.P. treatment. The Lady Mayoress saw that she was given tea, in the housekeeper's room, and next day, at the Exhibition, more excitement awaited her, as she was introduced to the Queen and Prince Albert.

Press descriptions of Mary were quite flattering: 'She possesses her faculties unimpaired; is very cheerful, has a considerable amount of humour in her composition; and is withal a woman of strong common sense, and frequently makes remarks that are very shrewd, when her great age and defective education are taken into account. She is fully aware that she has made herself somewhat famous; and among other things which she contemplates, is her return to Cornwall, to end her days in 'Paul Parish,' where she wishes to be interred, by the side of old Dolly Pentreath, who was also a native of Paul, and died at the age of 102 years.' Dolly Pentreath was the last native speaker of Cornish, like Mary she was a fish-wife, and died a year after Mary was born.

No doubt, Mary went home a great deal more quickly than she came to London. Probably it was by the new-fangled railway. Third class fares had been fixed by the government at 1d. per mile, so she had received, in the Mayor's largesse, more than enough to take her the two hundred miles to Plymouth. A badly sprung, unglazed carriage, with wooden seats, might have had its drawbacks, but as she sped homewards, in hours rather than weeks, she would have remembered a common westcountry saying, 'Third class ridin' be better'n first class walkin'.'

She survived another four years, to tell the wondrous tale of how she had been to London to see the Queen, as well as the Prince Consort and his Exhibition. She died in Penzance, on 5th December, 1855. They did not carry her the few miles to lie beside Dolly Pentreath in Paul Parish, she rests in St. Mary's Church- yard Penzance. Perhaps her name ought to have been included in some 'Book of Records' for I doubt if another octogenarian has equalled Mary's marathon.

Ann Glanville of Saltash

'Saltash,' wrote a contributor to Doidge's Annual who visited the town in 1879, 'is rapidly assuming a position that will give it a character throughout the country, in spite of what has been said about its water, gas and sewerage.'

The population was then increasing steadily, as it had done in the 20 years since Brunel bridged the Tamar and the rail link had brought a 'better class' of person to settle there.

He drew a word picture of his 'peep through garden railings' to see 'an aged man with snow white hair, reclining upon a rustic garden chair, watching a little girl playing with a tiny dog, with a blue silk ribbon and a bell attached to its neck. At another part of the garden sat a lady with two boys of seven and nine years respectively; one was reading, the other was assisting her in arranging a bouquet of wild flowers he had gathered with a servant in the lane'.

After spotting the postman with a letter from overseas, his conclusion was: 'This was the villa residence of some army or navy officer on a foreign station'. It must have been a very prolonged peep the writer took!

He had a word with that important citizen, the stationmaster, (whose opinion was that the population would double in 10 years) before taking 'a stroll about the town and a glimpse at the improved style of the shops', confirming his opinion that the town was on the 'up and up'.

He conceded that 'the peculiar character of Saltash proper' was preserved in the vicinity of the landing places at the bottom of the hill.

Here lived the ladies who gathered, boiled and pickled cockles.

Ann Glanville

Their street cry of 'Will 'ee buy any pickle-cocks' gave the town its nickname of Pickle-Cock Hill.

They also were ferrywomen, rowing passengers and goods across the Tamar.

Brunel's railway bridge, over which foot passengers were allowed to walk for 3d must have hit their trade.

The women were famed for 'powers of physical endurance and their natural tendency to masculine hardihood'.

This was demonstrated at regattas when their 'gigs shot around the course like birds and occasionally an event ended in a free fight. Those who came to pacify them came in for clouts and scratches'.

From their ranks came the celebrated Ann Glanville, who won the Devonport and Saltash Regatta rowing prize for 27 consecutive years, and also led her crew of women to victories at regattas in almost every British port. At Fleetwood, Queen Victoria complimented her especially.

She took the gig, named after her and crewed mostly by female relatives, across the Channel to Le Havre to rout a male crew before a crowd of 20,000.

Curiosities

The 'tanned and sinewy ladies' from Saltash were toasted in champagne by French Watermen.

This was in 1833 when she was 37 years of age.

The writer recalled a visit he made to her home when she was over 80. He accompanied a London merchant, who remembered her having 'ducked him in the sea and washed and dressed him at a very early age'.

He entered a room which had a stone floor. A four-post bed stood in the corner with a scrupulously clean white counterpane.

Old-fashioned photographs in Dutch metal frames covered the whitewashed wall over the mantelpiece. A large Bible which recorded the birth of members of the family in the early part of the last (ie 18th) century lay on a small table near the window.

Further over in the corner was another table covered with shells, silver medals, Chinese curiosities and family heirlooms.

Her memory was marvellous. She could relate incidents which occurred in the reign of George III and remember when Saltash sent two members to Parliament.

She also recalled that it's corporation exercised extensive rights over Plymouth Sound and the Hamoaze etc. and that the silver oar of the Mayor of Saltash was necessary in all cases of arrest.

In more recent times she had lit Mr Brunel's cigar (his trademark long before Churchill's) many a time. She had shaken the Prince-Consort's hand when he opened the bridge. She could also recall 'doing a reel' for the Duke of Edinburgh (Victoria's second son) when his ship, the Galatea, was laid up in Saltash.

The old lady was overwhelmed when her London visitor, on leaving, pressed a five pound note into her hand.

She married 'comparatively early in life, a man several years her junior'. Together they worked up quite a good business on the river and owned their own boat. Altogether they had 14 children. When her husband was ill for over a year Ann carried on alone to support the family.

Someone remembered her, at this time, 'bringing as many as 80 bags of corn in her boat from Sutton Pool, pulling the great cargo alone to Butt's Head Mill, two miles above Saltash.'

Ann's prowess as an oarswoman gave her the status of a modern Olympic champion but there was no sponsorship money to go with it.

There were though other rewards, as when the Prince of Wales and Duke of Edinburgh came to Plymouth to lay the foundation stone of the new Eddystone Lighthouse.

Connection

On a Sunday morning a steam launch was sent to Saltash to take Ann out to the Royal Yacht to be introduced to their Royal Highnesses and to dine with them.

Not at all overawed, Ann cracked a joke with the princes, and, as she said 'had a hearty good laugh with them'.

Ann had a close connection with the Royal Navy, one of her sons sailed on the Galatea and she was a mother-figure to any sailor based in Plymouth 'whatever trouble Jack got into when ashore, he never wanted for a "backer", if Ann Glanville was near'.

When she died a Royal Marines band played at her funeral.

Saltash has an Albert Road, named after the prince who greeted her and a Brunel Road after another of her heroes. Fittingly there is too a Glanville Terrace.

The Mad Messiah

The 'Second Coming' of Christ has been a persistent theme since the first century, when many believers expected it within their own lifetimes. Since then there has been a literally unending series of 'false Messiahs.'

In 1799, at St Columb, in Cornwall, was born John Nichols Tom, one of the more deluded and dangerous examples. His father was the landlord of the 'Joiner's Arms,' he had married a lady called Charity Bray. She soon showed signs of mental instability, and in those cruder times was known locally as 'Cracked Charity.'

Though mischievous (at the 'dame school' he cut off the whiskers of the dame's pet cat,) and with a pronounced streak of vanity, he was no dullard, and eventually was employed in an attorney's office, without any complaint from his employer.

This phase ended abruptly, when the inn, where he still lived with his parents, was burnt to the ground, and his poor mother was so affected as to be taken off to Bodmin Asylum, where she died. His father, having collected the insurance money, then married the schoolmistress who lived across the road, and John felt it would be the best thing to make a fresh start, elsewhere.

In what appeared a setback to his career, he took a job as cellarman to a wine merchant and maltster in Truro. When this firm ceased trading, he showed initiative by setting up as a maltster himself. Having married a Truro girl, he rebuilt her father's dilapidated old house and erected a malt house behind it. Almost immediately it, like the inn at St. Columb, was burnt to the ground. There were dark hints about an insurance fraud,

*Percy Honeywood Courtenay, Knight of Malta, etc., etc.,
as he appeared at the Election in 1832*

but a close check of the premises satisfied the insurers, who paid out a considerable £3,000, and John continued in business.

Soon however, people began to think 'there was a screw loose somewhere.' He affected the most outlandish clothes, and developed into an able orator, denouncing in public the Church, the aristocracy, and all organised government.

Then, his behaviour dispelled all doubts. At Bristol, having concluded a very successful deal, and collected a large sum of money, he wrote to his wife a perfectly normal letter, with some business instructions, and including the phrase: 'I am well and in good spirits (thank God for it).' It was the last time she heard from him, and the last he was to sign in his own name.

The key to what followed was his reading an account of the career of Lady Hester Stanhope. At 27, she had taken on the duties of mistress of the household of the Prime Minister, her bachelor uncle, William Pitt. As his confidante she was at the centre of national affairs. When, three years later, in 1806, he died, and a life devoid of such excitement and influence bored her, she went to Lebanon, and interfered in local politics, setting herself up as a kind of Queen and prophetess, she had great influence over the Arab population. She declared that the return of Christ was imminent and began making preparations for the start of the Millenium.

John Nichols Tom's imagination took over. He sailed for Lebanon, and told the British Consul at Beirut that he was Sir William Courtenay, Earl of Devon, asking him for an escort to Lady Stanhope's residence. That amused official, thinking it would be interesting to 'send one madhead to another,' obliged him. He was quickly seen to be a fraud, and Lady Stanhope did not admit him to explain to her that he was the herald, sent like a second John the Baptist, to be the forerunner of the returning Messiah.

Sailing home, via Malta, he landed in England as 'Sir William Percy Honeywood Courtenay, Knight of Malta, King of Jerusalem, and Prince of Abyssinia. As such, and in appropriate costume, he stood as a candidate for Parliament, at Canterbury, in December 1832. It says much for his acting ability that he got a substantial vote, and that many local ladies were eyeing him as a prospective husband for their daughters.

A brief foray into Devon, to claim his 'ancestral lands,' ended abruptly when the steward of the real Earl Courtenay warned him of the consequences of coming anywhere near Powderham Castle. On his return to Kent, he was committed to an asylum.

Here, he stayed for four years, until released by the intervention of Home Secretary Lord John Russell, who thought to gain electoral advantage in Cornwall by acceding to the pleas of his family and friends. He then went straight back to the Canterbury area and employed his rabble rousing skills among the poorer peasantry, who expected great things of him, including free land.

His ultimate ploy was to claim indeed to be Jesus Christ Himself, returned to earth. He painted on the wounds in his hands and side to prove it! Astonishingly he attracted a growing band of fanatical 'worshippers.' Tragedy came when a farmer, angry that his men had left their work to follow him, induced a magistrate to send constables to arrest him. He shot one constable dead and hacked at the body with a sword, explaining to his followers that he was 'executing the justice of Heaven.' He then retreated into a wood with forty followers. Here he administered a 'last supper' of bread and water, and assured them that all who believed in him were invulnerable.

When, inevitably, the soldiers came, the 'mad Messiah' shot dead the young Lieutenant who came forward to reason with them. The troops returned fire and he, with eight of his followers fell dead, they were armed only with sickles. The rest were taken prisoner, and at the Assizes of August 1838, ten were found guilty of murder and condemned to death, but, mercifully the sentences were commuted, some to transportation, and in one case to just one year's hard labour.

Hung, Drawn, and Quartered

'Hung, drawn, and quartered,' even in these video-nasty times, there is still a chilling finality about these words. For Plymothians, in the Tudor era, mere hangings were commonplace, and the 'gibbet on the Hawe' was frequently used to despatch a variety of offenders, from pickpockets to murderers. The awesome ritual summarised in the three deadly words was, in truth, a political deterrent, for then even the most popular monarch accepted that his reign had to be underpinned by terror.

The town treasurer's account book gives us interesting information about one such occasion, in April 1547. He does not give the name of the unfortunate principal in the gruesome drama, he is referred to as the 'Traytor of Cornewall,' but we do know the occasion that brought him to his sorry end. The 'Reformation' had just reached England, and, by act of parliament, the Latin Mass in churches had been superseded by the English Prayer-book, much the same one that is still in use today. To the many Cornishmen who, at this time, still spoke only Cornish, to hear the service in English was to hear it in the language of a foreign ruler. Cornwall had been Christian while England was still pagan. More than twelve centuries of worship in the Latin tongue meant that although the Cornish did not understand the actual words, they were comforting in their familiarity, and had a 'magic' entirely absent from the English of their overlords. So, indignant parishioners forced the clergy to go back to the old order of service, and once more the churches were filled with the smell of incense and the familiar cadences of the Latin Mass.

What made matters more serious was that members of the local gentry, who had tried to enforce the will of King Edward VI, and his parliament in this matter, were attacked in their homes by bloodthirsty mobs. The old records called it 'The time of Commocions.' It had to be stopped and soldiers were sent into Cornwall to enforce the law. The treasurer's book shows that, on 8th April, one Henry Blase received payment: 'For hym and his companye, when they rode into Cornewall agaynst the rebells there.' They had brought back to Plymouth with them the luckless 'traytor' who was to be made an example of, as the subject of a 'set piece' execution.

It was, for some, a quite jolly occasion. We see an entry of a payment to 'William Bickford, for wyne at receiving of the traytor of Cornewall.' Others were to profit from the poor chap's downfall, chiefly executioner John Wylstreme, who was paid six shillings (say £50 today). He had a messy and complicated ritual to perform. First the hanging, then disembowelling, and finally the head, arms, and legs were detached (these were the 'quarters') for exhibition in various places. John Matthew was, in this case, paid for 'Caryinge a Qtr. of the traytor to Tavistock.' To preclude any possibility of honourable burial, the left over bits were ceremoniously burnt. There is an entry of payment for: 'A dowzen of faggots.' Timber for the gallows cost 12d., and 4d. was paid to the man who led the horse drawing the prisoner on his last bumpy ride (on a hurdle) from the town 'clink' to the Hoe. There is some evidence that it was a special occasion, as the treasurer had to pay for: 'poles to put ye head and quarter of ye said traytor upon, and two cramps of ieron for to stay ye poles upon ye Gyld Hall.' With so explicit a warning to Plymothians, it is no wonder that the 'Commocions' did not extend across the Tamar!

Hasty Marriage led To Gallows

In real life, just as in fiction, tragedy and comedy are often interwoven, and the life of Jonathan Simpson is a good example of this.

He was born in Launceston, in 1654, when Cromwell's government held sway over the mostly reluctant Cornish. There is no reason to believe that his father took any risks to aid the King, for he prospered throughout the period, and was described as 'well off,' when he apprenticed the 14 year old Jonathan to a Bristol linen draper.

Possibly his father would have been a little worried about a youth so far from home, in those heady Restoration days, when 'Merry Monarch' Charles II was setting a none too elevated tone for society. He however proved to be both steady and industrious, and at 21, having finished his apprenticeship, was given £1,500 by his father to set him up in business, in Bristol.

Now, however, the course of his life started almost to resemble a 'restoration farce.' It was not that the young man did not have an eye for business, as indeed he also had for a pretty girl, but unfortunately he thought he saw a simple way of 'killing two birds with one stone.' He made the acquaintance of a pretty girl, with the added attraction of 'two thousand pounds of her own.' Her parents were more than willing to entertain a match, even though the young lady had already 'engaged herself to a young man of small means,' and insisted on her marrying Simpson. She showed her open resentment from the start of her marriage.

Her former young man, in a fit of disgust at his rejection, had also married, but Simpson found out that they still wrote to each other. Determined to discover if she was having an affair, he told her he was going away for a fortnight to visit his relatives at Launceston.

As soon as he had cleared his heels, his wife invited her former sweetheart around for an intimate supper of chicken and wine. Simpson, who had never left Bristol, burst into the house and made for the dining room. The young man was just able to scramble into a large chest before he entered. Simpson, who had spotted a movement of the lid of the chest, kept cool, and complimented his wife on the excellent meal on the table, then sent her on a contrived errand to a distant street. He then dispatched a servant to bring the young man's wife to the house. When she entered, he lifted the lid of the chest, and much enjoyed the 'ructions' that followed.

With an unfaithful wife (long before the days of divorce) he took drastic action. He threw out his wife from the home, selling both house and business, with £5,000 (every penny he had) he left Bristol for ever. Over the next eighteen months, he spent it all, living riotously in London. It was a merry life that proved to be a rather short one.

To obtain the funds to live as he had become accustomed, he took to the roads, as a highwayman. After only a brief apprenticeship to that trade, he found himself in the dock at the Old Bailey, and condemned to death. By bribery, and every other form of persuasion, his family in Cornwall got him a reprieve. He was at Tyburn, with the rope around his neck, when it arrived.

As, riding behind one of the sheriff's officers back to Newgate Prison, he was asked if he had thought of a reprieve, as he stood on the scaffold, he quipped: 'No more than I thought of my dying day.' His high spirits were not diminished when he reached the gaol, for the 'turnkey' who had seen him off to die, said he had no authority to take him in without a fresh warrant, and let him go free. 'Well,' said Simpson 'what an unhappy dog am I! That Tyburn and Newgate in one day refuse to entertain me. I'll see if I cannot merit a reception at both, next time I am brought hither.'

Within six weeks, he had committed forty more robberies. In the winter of that year the Thames froze over, and, as an expert skater, he took to the river instead of the road, kicking up the heels of rich looking skaters and robbing them at leisure as they sprawled on the ice.

Returning to the highways, he on one occasion held up a coach and was handed a heavy silk purse, which, in his room at an inn later, he opened to find only brass tokens, used in playing cards. Four months later, he lay in wait for the same gentleman, on Bagshot Heath. Stopping his carriage, he put a pistol to his head and said: 'Sir, I believe you made a mistake last time I saw you, in giving me these. I have been troubled ever since that you wanted these counters at cards, and I return them. For my care however, I require you to get out and give me your breeches, that I may search them at leisure.' The embarrassed victim had to comply, and Simpson took his breeches to his hideout, to find a gold watch, a gold snuff box, and a purse with 98 guineas.

To rob Lord Delamere, he employed a sly trick. He rode up to the coach, which was attended by armed servants, and declared that he had been waylaid and robbed by two rogues a little way down the road. Lord Delamere sent his men off to catch the thieves, and for his kindness was then robbed of £40.

The end of the story came when he attempted to rob two gentlemen who turned out to be army officers. In a desperate fight, the highwayman almost got away, but one of the wounded officers shot his horse, which falling on him, held him pinned down until captured. Wounded in both arms and one leg, he arrived at Newgate, which this time received him without demur, as did the hangman at Tyburn, where, in his 33rd year, he was hanged, on Sep. 8th, 1686.

John Passmore Edwards
Practical Philanthropist

The Victorians left us an inheritance of public buildings such as hospitals and libraries, many provided by private benefactions and still used to this day.

One philanthropist in this field was Cornish-born John Passmore Edwards, whose creed was quite a simple one.

'As I had accumulated mainly by the labour of others, I thought, and think, it was only reasonable and just that others should share in the garnered result.

'I also thought, and think, that the great working class—the foundation and bulwark of national existence, and the chief producer of national necessities—are entitled to primary consideration.

'I consequently decided to do what I could for their welfare, and thought the best thing to do was to help them help each other; and that this could be most productively done by promoting institutional activity.'

To use the expressive vulgarism he certainly 'put his money where his mouth was.' He built 72 such institutions, 23 libraries, as well as hospitals, convalescent homes, technical schools, children's homes, and village halls.

Most compassionately he remembered one of the most helpless, and almost despised classics of that time, epileptics, for whom he provided, at Chalfont, separate homes for men and boys, and women and girls.

The majority of the other institutions were sited in Devon and Cornwall and extensively in the East End of London, an area he became familiar with in his many years in Fleet Street as a newspaper proprietor.

Village Hall

His very first benefection was a village hall for Blackwater, near Redruth, where he was born 14 years before Victoria came to the throne. His father, a market gardener, was also a Calvinistic Methodist lay preacher. His mother (born Susan Passmore) was from a Newton Abbot Baptist family.

He received his early, very elementary, education at the village school and recalled later that he had sold strawberries in Redruth market to help pay the 2d a week fee.

Strawberries figure also in a very amusing and revealing passage in his autobiography. It seems that as a 12-year-old in the top class of the village school he was so 'smitten' by a girl of the same age as to be altogether distracted from his lessons.

He would in the evenings take the very best strawberries from his father's garden to her wrapped up in a cabbage leaf: 'For a year or two before I left school, and some time afterwards, she was the Goddess of my idolatry' he wrote.

She however did not reciprocate his affection and when he sent her love letters her big brother threatened him with a thrashing.

When he left school he continued his education at evening classes and by voracious reading of any book or magazine he could scrape together a few pennies to buy.

Never lacking self-confidence at 17 he was lecturing on politics and social problems to the St Agnes Literary Society. He was strongly against the 'Corn Laws' which, in the 'Hungry Forties' enforced a tax on imported grain, making even barley bread reach famine prices for the poor.

Later he was an advocate of universal education, non-intervention in foreign wars—he called the Crimean War a 'Blunder and a Crime,'—and the protection of trade unions against crippling damages claims. He also supported the abolition of blood sports, and the abolition of capital punishment. As a youth he had seen a public hanging outside Bodmin jail and his

FREE LIBRARY, REDRUTH.

PASSMORE EDWARDS FREE LIBRARY

Redruth Library

father had thrashed him for leaving his work to walk the 22 miles to see this spectacle.

At the age of 20 he escaped from the market garden to work as a clerk in a lawyer's office, at £10 an annum. He came home at weekends, but had to be up at 5 am on Mondays to walk to work in Truro seven miles away.

He would carry with him three of his mother's pasties, his dinner for the first half of the week, three more came with the carrier on Thursdays!

Real freedom and the fulfilment of his great ambition came when he got a post as reporter on the Manchester Sentinel, at £40 a year. The radical paper soon failed, but the experience stood him in good stead when he went to London and Fleet Street.

There he augmented his writing income by lecturing for progressive causes. Futile attempts to start publishing his own journals with very little capital led to bankruptcy. But when discharged he took over an ailing trade paper 'Building News' and began to make a profit.

After paying all his former creditors in full, he purchased another 'lame duck,' a half-penny newspaper called the London Echo, which became so successful as to lay the basis of a publishing fortune.

He had some political ambitions and in 1868 unsuccessfully contested Truro, but in 1880 he was elected as a Liberal for Salisbury.

Gradually be came to despair of any rapid reform of working class conditions through Parliament, and, after 1895, concentrated on his own social and educational programme.

He wanted to do something for his mother's birthplace, Newton Abbot, and first thought of a hospital, but found there was already one there so instead provided a library and technical school.

When, aged 79, he came to lay the foundation stone, he was so overcome by emotion at the thought of his mother's childhood of comparative poverty only a hundred yards from the spot, he could not continue his speech.

His libraries and hospitals ensure that he will not be forgotten, and, as he intended, kindred spirits of succeeding generations will never lack the books he so treasured.

The Merry Mayor of Bodmin

'Laugh and grow fat,' is an almost forgotten proverb, though those grim and gloomy 'joggers' that we now see pounding the pavements, still seem to regard it as a dire warning! Grow fat and make other people laugh, does seem to get a little nearer the truth (illustrated in its crudest aspect by the seaside postcard) and, through the ages, we can observe the joviality and popularity of corpulent clowns, from Sir John Falstaff to Sir Harry Secombe, who, perhaps defensively, have managed to blur the line between 'laughing at' and 'laughing with.'

Mayor William Robert Hicks, of Bodmin, born on April 1, 1808, reached in his prime a height of just over five feet and a weight of just under sixteen stones, and so comes easily into the 'corpulent' category, and though only his few enemies would have called this conscientious public man a clown, he did enjoy jokes of the unsophisticated, and sometimes crude, variety, current in the Cornish countryside. Despite the birthdate, he was nobody's fool, but a clear-headed businessman. He was also a good mathematician, and a quite capable violinist. He, said a contemporary, 'possessed the art and power to tell a story with his countenance as with his voice. Indeed the alterations of mood in his face were like a musical accompaniment to a song.' He met a fellow spirit in George Wightwick, a Plymouth architect, and, through him, was invited to many of the great country houses in Devon and Cornwall (they were particularly welcome at Mount Edgecumbe) where they would tell stories, and sing, accompanying themselves on the violin. When one of his admirers took Hicks to his London Club, to divert his dining companions, his homely humour fell terribly flat, for most of his stories had a

William R. Hicks

mid-Cornish setting and owed a great deal of their effect to dialect.

Some of his stories, which concerned mental illness, might nowadays be considered in bad taste, but he was a kindly and progressive man. It was a lucky day for the inmates when, in 1848, he was made Governor of Bodmin Asylum, where, a nineteenth century writer reports, 'he found the old barbarous system of treatment of the insane in full swing.' He insisted on gentle methods, and physical restraint only when absolutely necessary for the patient's safety. He took a personal interest in one inmate, whom he found chained in a dark cell on a bed of straw, and nearly cured him by kindly treatment. He kept a caring eye on this man, 'Daniel', who seems to have possessed a great deal of shrewdness and native wit. A story Hicks loved to tell was of a gentleman who visited the asylum and said to Daniel, 'I hear man that you are Hicks's fool.' 'Aw,' replied Daniel, 'I zee you do your awn busines in that line!'

There is no doubt that Daniel had a very mischievous side to his character. Once, when he was asked where a certain path went, he answered, 'Zure I can't tell 'ee, I've nawed un bide 'ere this last twenty year.' That he was, as the Cornish say, more 'R' than 'F' (rogue than fool) is illustrated by the mischievous trick he played on the manager of a circus which was passing by the asylum wall. Daniel, sitting on the wall and inspecting the cavalcade, called out to him, ''Ow much might 'ee pay turnpike for they there spekkady 'osses?' 'Oh?' said the manager, 'the same as for the others.' 'Do 'ee now?' said Daniel. 'Well to be sure; my vather 'ad a spekkady 'oss that never paid no turnpike. They there sparky 'osses don't pay no turnpikes 'ere.' The manager asked eagerly, 'Am I to understand that piebald horses are exempt from paying at the toll gate?' He got the reply, 'What I zed I bides by. They there spekkady 'osses never pay no turnpikes 'ere in Cornwall. What they may do elsewhere, I can't zay.' The manager swallowed the story, and Daniel watched him ride down to the turnpike gate, and enjoyed, from a distance, the argument with its custodian which followed. When the manager galloped back up the road to berate him, saying, 'What do you mean by telling me that, in Cornwall, piebald horses pay no turnpike?' Daniel shouted, as he jumped prudently behind the wall, 'That's right, 'cos you 'ave to pay it for 'em!'

Some of Hicks's asylum jokes would, today, be called 'black' or 'sick' comedy. He told how a harmless inmate was set to watch, through a peep-hole, a violent lunatic, who was plunging and kicking wildly in a padded cell. The poor chap calling for the release of death, shouted, 'Oh, I wish I was in Abraham's bosom!' The man outside then shouted through the peep-hole, 'Why, I tell 'ee if you was, you'd kick the guts out of 'en.' Another shocker is Hicks's story of how he met an acquaintance one morning, in Bodmin, and remarked that he did not look at all well. The man said that he had spent an indifferent night, and his explanation, which Hicks would faithfully mimic, went as follows: 'I sleep with father, and I woke up, all in the dead waste and middle of the night, had I reached forth my hand and couldn't feel nothing: so I sez, sez I, "Wherever is my poor dear old aged tender parent," I got out of bed and strick a light and sarched the room; sarched under the bed and in the cupboards; and sez I, "Wherever is my poor dear old aged tender parent?" Then I went to the coal hole and sarched about, all in the dead waste and middle of the night, and sarched all about; and sez I, "Wherever is my poor dear old aged tender parent?" And I went down into the garden, all in the dead waste and middle of the night; and sez I, "Wherever is my poor dear old aged tender parent?" I went down to the parzley bed, and there I found 'en. He'd a cut his throt with the rape (reaping) hook. I took 'en by the hair on his head, and I zaid, sez I, "You darned old grizzley blackguard, you've brought disgrace on the family." I brought 'en in, and laid 'un on the table, and runned for the doctor: and he zewed up the throt o'un avore the vital spark was extinct. Zo you zee, Mr. Hicks, I've had rather an indiffer'nt night.'

In lighter, if only slightly more tasteful vein, was his account of the curate who tried to teach a boy, in Sunday school, his duty to his parents: 'What do you owe your mother, Bill Lemon?' 'I don't owe her nothin'! her never lent me nothin'.' 'But she takes care of you.' The boy stared. 'What does she do for you?' 'Her gives me a scat in the vace sometimes and tells me to go to h—', the curate cut him short. 'That is not what I mean. When you are sick, what does she do?' the lad hesitated, 'Wipes it op,' he replied.

Hicks did not mind a laugh at his own expense. Once, when at a civic dinner the butler announced 'The Mayor of Bodmin,' he, indicating his bulging waistline, added 'and his corporation.' When however, an admirer took him to his London club, to divert the company at dinner, his jokes, with their mid-Cornish setting and dialect fell flat with such a sophisticated audience. There was an embarrassed silence, when he might have recalled the tale he used to tell of farmer Polkinghorne. The farmer was visited by a parliamentary candidate's wife, canvassing his vote. She gushingly said, 'When you come up to town, do come and see us, come any time, come to dinner.' Zechariah Polkinghorne took her at her word, and when in London on business, knocked at her door. Concealing her consternation, for fear of losing the votes of Zechariah and his friends, she led him to the dining table. He sat, ill at ease among the fashionable guests, and when the hostess apologised for not being able, at such short notice, to pair him with a lady, he replied, 'Never mind ma'am, it doth remind me of my old sow. Her had thirteen little zuckers (piglets) in the brood, and only twelve little contrivances for 'em to zuck to.' The startled lady thought she had better say something, and enquired, 'What did the thirteenth do Mr. Polkinghorne?' 'Why ma'am,' answered the farmer, 'thickey there little zucker was like me now—just out in the cold.'

The church was the source of several of Hicks's stories. A Tavistock man was reported to have said to his vicar, concerning a girl with whom he was keeping company, 'Pa'sson, promise never to marry me to thickey there maid, when I be drunk.' The parson, slightly shaken, agreed, and was more shocked by the 'follow-up,' 'for I'll take damned good care you never do it when I'm sober!' On much the same theme was his story of the little boy in church, who, hearing the banns called 'for the third time of asking,' said, in an audible voice, to his mother, 'I shouldn't like it to be called out in church that sister Jane had been asking for a husband three times afore her got one.'

That some things have changed very little in the past hundred years or so is illustrated by the story of the boy who was asked, 'Where be you abound to this afternoon?' 'Gwain to zee the vootball match,' was his reply. 'Aw! Like to be a good 'en?' said his friend. 'Yes I reckon, there be a lot o' bitter feelin' betwixt the two teams,' he answered.

Hicks died, in Bodmin, in September 1868, aged 60, not a long life, but assuredly a merry one.

Report From America—1812

Alistair Cooke's weekly radio report from America has long been a national institution, and no doubt, one day, the recordings will be part of the vast archives built up since the invention of radio and television. How meagre in comparison are the eyewitness accounts from past times. Fortunately there survives a record made, in 1812, of an itinerary worthy of Mr. Cooke's reporting, had he been alive then.

In a year when the Napoleonic War had forced up grain prices to famine levels, and there was food rioting from Plymouth to Penzance, radical Cornish farmer James Hoskin determined to see what opportunity there was for westcountry immigrants in the United States. A poor man in early life, he had, by years of toil, reclaimed a farm from the rough moorland slopes of Castel-an-Dinas, an ancient hill fort in the Parish of Ludgvan, near Penzance. He was 50 years old, when, on Sept. 28, 1810, he sailed from Penzance on the American schooner 'Packet of Boston,' bound for New York with a mixed cargo.

At this time, relations between Britain and the infant U.S.A. were tense, as the chagrin of defeat in the War of Independence was compounded by what Britain looked on as blockade running by American vessels bound for France. Hoskin, who was not unsympathetic to the aims of either the American or the French revolutions was surprised, but quite pleased, when the departing vessel, bearing the 'Stars and Stripes,' was cheered from the shore by Cornish dock workers.

After a rough seven weeks at sea, the Packet of Boston reached the island, off Massachusetts, still known as 'Martha's Vineyard,' where James had a welcome break on shore. He was overwhelmed by his first taste of American prosperity, and by their lack of snobbery. He wrote: 'We put up at Dr. Spalding's tavern, a handsome house. Our host was a doctor, a justice of the peace, and a tavern keeper, but quite the gantleman. The family at mealtime sat down with us—this is the American fashion. With our tea we had plenty of beefsteaks, boiled eggs, preserved fruit, hot cakes etc. We paid a dollar a day (bed included,) but all through America we saw nothing of those pests of beggars, waiters, chambermaids, coachmen, postboys etc., which constantly harass, and insult, the traveller in England.

On docking in New York, there was trouble with the captain. Hoskin had bought a quantity of earthenware at Penzance, to sell at a profit in America, but the captain had taken it off his hands at what he thought a fair price, promising him to pay cash in New York. However he now refused to pay Hoskin a penny, and what is more, disposed of the goods to a merchant. It was only when Hoskin got the merchant to help him in complaining to the authorities that he got his money.

The captain of the vessel in which he sailed from New York to Washington was an even greater villain. He watched him, in a drunken rage beating the old negro cook. Shouting 'Damn the negroes, I hate them,' he flogged him with a heavy stick, a piece of rope, and finally the galley's fire shovel.

The Cornishman, taking pity on the cook, offered to do his work if the captain would leave him alone. When, within hours, the cook died, the captain menacingly asked Hoskin what he thought was the cause of his death. He avoided answering, but did not report the affair when he got to Washington. He wrote that the mate would have sworn in the captain's favour, and that he could do no good for the dead cook.

On the run up the Potomac, he went ashore for a while, and was impressed with: 'the happiness of the farmers in this place, which flowed in the abundance of the first necessities of life, their wants few and easily supplied; no cares about rent, all being peace, plenty, and happiness around them.'

He gives only one instance of anti-English feeling. A young woman he met on Long Island, whose brother had been grabbed by the press gang, for the British Navy, while ashore in England, declared, (with obvious sympathy for the French) 'I wish the English were guillotined!'

He described a voyage up the Delaware, when for the first time he saw a steam boat, travelling on a paddle steamer built by the American Engineer, Robert Fulton. It went 'a full five miles an hour against wind and tide, was wide and roomy, and a tavern kept on board, and passage very cheap.'

While in New York he had witnessed an event of some historic importance, Fulton's first trial of the torpedo, which was his invention. He tried it out against an American brig-of-war, the captain of which had 'prepared a defence by casting a net round the ship to prevent the torpedo diving under.' Happily for any skeleton crew left aboard, the defence succeeded!

The name of the brig was the 'Argus.' Later that year (1812) when war had broken out with America, the Argus was, after a bitter engagement, brought into Plymouth as a prize. Her Captain, William Henry Allen, lost a leg and died ashore of wounds. It is he, and one of his midshipmen, who are still remembered, on the carefully kept headstone, by the 'Door of Unity' of the Prysten House.

On the outbreak of hostilities, Hoskin had just managed to get home to Cornwall, it was a quick, if again rough, passage driven on by westerly gales. He died in 1823, but was not buried in Ludgvan Churchyard. In his youth, he was said to have 'kissed the parson's wife,' the reverend gentleman swore that if he survived him he would only bury him in the remotest corner of the churchyard. James scorned the thought, and was buried in unconsecrated ground, on the hill farm he had won from the moor.

Dukes and the Duchy

From the Norman Conquest, Cornwall was an Earldom, but, in 1334, King Edward III's brother, the boy Earl John, died and the title was in abeyance for three years.

On March 17th 1337, the king, noticing a 'great falling off in the names and honours and dignity of rank, as by failures of issue, and from other events,' created his eldest son Duke of Cornwall.

The new Duchy had much the same boundaries as the former Earldom. The Duke was only seven, but the complicated manoeuvrings of dynastic politics disregarded age. Indeed, only one month after his birth, negotiations were afoot to marry him to a French princess, at three years old he had been made Earl of Chester. It was a world in which births, marriages, and deaths could follow in very quick succession.

Even more than the present Duke, he merits the name 'Action Man.'

At 16, he 'won his spurs' in hand-to-hand combat at Crecy, and developed into a mighty warrior, the scourge of the French.

From the colour of his splendid suit of armour, he was known and feared by them as the 'Black Prince.'

In 1356, he was in Plymouth, staying at Plympton Priory. With his many retainers he helped to 'eat the monks out of house and home,' as the huge expedition of 300 ships awaited a fair wind for France.

The next year, following the epic victory of Poitiers, he returned bringing with him as prisoner King John of France, who started on the road from Plymouth to London mounted on a white charger. Twenty years later he returned to Plymouth after a far less glorious campaign, dying of consumption, at 47.

There have been 24 Dukes of Cornwall since him, ten including three infants, who lived only for days, did not succeed to the throne. There is only a Duke of Cornwall when there is a sovereign with a son, in the interim periods the Duchy revenues revert to the Crown.

The revenue aspect is important, the Dukedom was no empty honour. In the founding charter, mention is made of Cornwall's then very productive tin mines.

The revenues from these mines were paid direct to the Duchy by the miners, in return for which they were granted self-government by their own Stannary parliament and courts.

This, together with manorial dues, made the heir to the throne financially independent and had important political consequences.

There has, only recently, been some disquiet among Cornish farmers about proposed increases of Duchy rents. It is a subject, together with conditions of tenure, that has cropped up regularly over the centuries.

From early times, it was the custom for lands to be leased for seven-year periods, renewal being effected on payment of an appropriate sum at a 'Court of Assession.'

In 1844, an act was passed which allowed those who could show a continuous occupation for 60 years to convert their tenure to a virtual freehold, only paying a very small 'commuted rent' annually, though not so small as those purely nominal 'peppercorn' rents paid by some manors.

There are amusing varieties of these, including: Yearly rents of one greyhound, or a garland of roses, even a single red rose, or a single grain of wheat.

A cottage near Constantine Church paid a pie of limpets, raisins and herbs. There also crept in, in the mid nineteenth century, the wide-spread Cornish practice of letting lands on a lease of three lives. After payment of a fairly substantial capital sum, no further revenue came to the Duchy until the death of the last of the three people nominated, and as one was usually very young, the Duchy, in particular the Duke who succeeded the original lessor, was often the loser.

It was typical of the businesslike Prince Albert, in control during the minority of the future Edward VII, that he put a stop to these practices.

This could have been resented, but when Prince Albert Edward came to Cornwall, as Duke in his own right, he was warmly welcomed, particular at St Columb Major, in May 1866, when he received an address from 138 racing enthusiasts thanking him for his patronage of the course.

From what we know now, he was probably as interested in the local 'fillies' as the horses, though at 25, he had been married three years to Alexandra his beautiful Danish bride, and had already ensured the succession with two sons, the Duke of Clarence who died 10 years before his father came to the throne, and Prince George who succeeded him, first as Duke of Cornwall, and later as George V.

He and succeeding Dukes made frequent visits to the Duchy, and as all have been 'sailor princes' these have usually conveniently fitted in with Naval occasions in Plymouth.

On the 600th anniversary of the Duchy Charter, in 1937, there was no Duke, but Edward VIII, who had relinquished the title on his accession the year before, visited the Duchy for a ceremony.

He did this by going down the road to Kennington, one of the Duchy's most valuable manors. Though far from Cornwall, it is one of the 'forinesca,' non-Cornish manors, of which there are others in Devon, Somerset, Dorset, Berkshire, Hertfordshire, Kent, Norfolk and Monmouth.

No one has taken so personal an interest in the Duchy as the present Duke. He has even gone to the extent of spending a 'holiday' mucking out and milking on a Duchy farm. It is also a possibility that he will equal, or even exceed, the 60-year tenure of the future Edward VII should his mother, like Victoria, celebrate her Diamond Jubilee in 2012.

Cornwall's Holy Wells
A Celtic Heritage

From pre-historic time, water has been worshipped as one of the 'elemental spirits,' along with earth, air, and fire. The symbolism has come down through the ages, and was adopted, and adapted, by the Christian tradition. As the well known hymn has it, the Church was created by 'Water and the Word.'

For centuries before Christianity came to the country, there were dozens of sacred springs and wells throughout Cornwall, to the waters of which magical and healing powers were attributed. When Celtic Christian monks came as missionaries, from Ireland, Wales and Brittany, in the 'Dark Ages,' they deliberately set up their hermitage cells close to these, firstly of course to have drinking water and water for baptism, but also gradually to substitute Christian beliefs and ceremonies for the immemorial pagan rites. The granite crosses have declared the intention, but age old traditions have never completely faded away.

St. Nunne's Well

This is at Altarnun, in the north of Cornwall, once one of the most famous of holy wells, it still bubbles away in a field to the south east of the church. The water comes out from under a grassy mound. In recent years some low brickwork has been placed around to prevent cattle fouling it, but all its former glory has departed. It was named in honour of the mother of St. David of Wales, from whom the village's name also derives. As locals will still tell you, its fame rested on the reputation of its waters being able to cure madness. In the sixteenth century, the water used to fall into a large and quite deep pit, with a low stone wall. The patient would be seated on this parapet, with his back to the water, and was precipitated into the pool by an unexpected push. He was then grabbed by two stalwart attendants, who 'dunked' him repeatedly, and then threw him (half drowned) onto the bank, to be hauled off to the church, for a special mass. Perhaps in some cases this primitive 'shock therapy' had a beneficial effect.

Holy Well Laneast

Three miles north of Altarnun is the well at Laneast, called by some local people 'The Jordan,' and by others, just the 'wishing well.' It is still visited by the occasional tourist. It was once used for baptisms, one old lady in 1890 remembered when water was

Holy Well, Laneast

fetched from it to fill the font in Laneast Church. There is no firm information as to which saint it was dedicated, but probably as in the case of the church it was St. Sidwell. The 16th century 'chapel,' is 6 ft. 8 ins. long and 6 ft. wide, with a round headed arch on the south, and a beautiful roof. There is an unlocked wooden door.

In the days before refrigeration, local farmers' wives would use the cold waters to chill their cream there in summer before making butter. The picture was drawn around 1890.

Holy Well, St. Breward

Holy Well St. Breward

To the south west of Laneast, ten miles across Bodmin Moor, is
St. Breward's holy well. Even as long ago as 1856, a visitor
reported it neglected and in poor shape, finding 'only a few pins
in the muddy bottom.' (This indicates that the ancient custom of
girls throwing bent pins into a holy well 'to bind their lovers to
them,' had not quite died out then.) A later report, in 1890, shows
there had been further deterioration, and some vandalism by
miners tapping the spring to supply their workings. They had
not however completely drained the spring. Though the observer
describes the 'chapel' as 'tottering' the drawing made about this
time does not indicate imminent collapse. No pins were discovered at this inspection. A twentieth century guide book
reports: 'The sturcture is dilapidated, but the arched entrance
remains, and there are vestiges nearby of ecclesiastical buildings,
possibly part of the destroyed Chapel of St. James. Originally the

Well of Mt. Edgcumbe

well had been dedicated to St. Michael and St. James, and the name of St. Breward was arbitrarily chosen by a later Lord of the Manor.

St. Julian's Well, Mount Edgcumbe

There are several holy wells almost up to the banks of the Tamar. One of the smallest is that of St. Julian at Mount-Edgcumbe. Inside it measures just 6ft. 3ins. by 4 ft. 9ins. Architecturally it is of the early 14th century. At the fountain end is a niche which probably contained a figure of the saint. The original jambs of the doorway, and the niches, are of a green freestone from Landrake parish. The rest of the masonry is of more local stone. There was a thin coating of plaster on the walls inside. The flooring was of red and green tiles, fragments of which have been found. The building was restored to the condition in the picture, in 1884, and remains intact.

The Well of St. Dominick

The 'Cornwall Directory' for 1938 states: By the side of the road leading from Chapel Farm to the Tamar is the holy well, at the back of which there is a niche. The whole of the structure is now much overgrown. The drawing shows it half a century earlier. In more recent times it was 'splendidly restored,' to be re-dedicated by Truro's Bishop Hunkin on 4th, Aug. 1951. It had originally been dedicated to St. Dominick in Oct. 1259 (It is not known exactly who he was.) It is now a stone and ribbed building, with a handsome wrought iron gate. There is a niche at the back, with a small statue of the Virgin Mary. Much of the ancient stonework is incorporated in the restored chapel. There is now very little water coming from the spring.

Holy Well, St. Dominick

Dupath Well

Dupath Well or Baptistry

Less that 2 miles south east of Callington, is Dupath Well, one of the most famous holy wells in Britain. Though only reached down a rough farm track this ancient oratory, with its granite gables and pinnacles almost hidden among the trees, has from time to time been restored, and has weathered the centuries well.

Known also as St. Ethelred's Chapel, it was a place of Christian baptism. Twelve feet square, and eighteen feet high, it looks more like a small church than a hermit's cell. This is though, a place where many of the old pre-Christian superstitions have lingered.

Here, by observing a certain ritual, one's future could be foretold, also the water was said to cure whooping cough, and to dispel evil spirits, if sprinkled on bewitched cattle. Here too girls threw pins into the water for romantic reasons.

There is a strange legend that a duel was fought alongside the well between one Gottlieb, a rich man, and Sir Colan, a poor, but handsome knight, for the hand of a 'fair wench.' The girls father preferred Gottlieb, she fancied the young knight. In the duel, both were fatally wounded. Perhaps they should have consulted the omens at the well before they started!

The legend explains the unusually ornate and substantial nature of the building by it having been erected, in memory of Sir Colan, by Githa (the fair wench in question), who spent the rest of her life there, praying for the repose of his soul.

St. Neot's Well

One of the most interesting of the wells in Mid-Cornwall is that of St. Neot. It is sited in a meadow below the church. Once pilgrims from the continent used to visit it, as it was credited with miraculous powers of healing. The small chapel over the well still exists, but the description in a guide book of fifty years ago, of three stone steps descending into a pool of limpid water, is no longer valid, in fact stagnant would be a more accurate word.

Legend has it that St. Neot, like Zaccheus, was of small stature, and had to stand on a stool to reach the altar. However some very

Well of St. Keyne

tall tales are told about him. One was that he would stand, up to his neck, in the water each morning while reciting prayers. Three tame trout swam around him while he did so. Every day St. Neot's servant would take one trout from the well and cook it for his master's dinner. The saint, having dined, would carefully scrape the bones off his platter back into the water, and, immediately, they became another lively, fat trout. It seems preposterous that even a medieval peasant should believe this, but after all he was enjoined to believe implicitly in the story of the loaves and fishes in the Bible, and of the miraculous catch in Galilee, so perhaps simple faith did stretch to it.

The Well of St. Keyne

Another well in the Liskeard area is that of St. Keyne. There is a legend that St. Keyne was the aunt of St. David Wales, so possibly a sister of St. Nunne. She is supposed to have presented this well to the villagers, in return for the church they had dedicated to her. It was believed that the first partner to drink from the waters (after marriage in the Church of St. Keyne) would thenceforth 'wear the trousers,' as the dominant partner. The story goes that one husband who rushed to the well, leaving his wife in the church porch, was fooled by a wily spouse, who had taken a bottle of the water to church with her! Here is the last verse from a ballad by the poet Southey:

> 'I hastened as soon as the wedding was o'er,
> And left my good wife in the porch,
> But i' faith she had been far wiser than I,
> For she took a bottle to church.'

The drawing shows the well in 1890. Nowadays the massive trees have gone, the cottage in the background has been demolished and the masonry is disjointed.

The Well of St. Cleer

Almost equidistant from Liskeard, but to the north, is the well of St. Cleer. It is seen, in 1890, in a ruinous state, though the ancient cross near the well, over seven feet high, and with a cross in relief on both sides still stands. There has since been some extensive reconstruction of the cross and the small chapel over the well, though little of the charm, and tangible sense of the past, conveyed by the earlier drawing has remained.

Already diminished was the Celtic connection, for, after the Norman Conquest, local landlord Ingelman de Bray transferred

Well of St. Cleer

its association, with a now unremembered saint, to one with St. Clair of Normandy.

St. Martin's Well

Is in Liskeard itself, and has the most romantic associations of all this group. Unlike St. Keyne's water, that from St. Martin's well does not promote married rivalries, but young couples about to marry used to stand on a stone beside the well, and drink the water, to ensure married bliss. According to some sources the name Liskeard means 'the place of sweethearts.'

Menacuddle Well, St. Austell

From its name this well also might be guessed to have romantic associations. Doubtless it has inspired many a giggle, as suc-

Menacuddle Well

ceeding generations of girls dropped their bent pins in, 'to bind their lovers to them.' Before English replaced the native language, this would not have been so, for 'maen' in Cornish means 'stone,' and 'guidhal' an Irishman. The Irishman's stone was possibly the Celtic cross erected near the well by a missionary monk.

St. Austell himself is said to have established his cell here. Not only was the well a baptistry, but sick children were bathed in its waters, and the sick washed their running sores, hoping for miraculous cures. It is an off-putting thought that others drank the waters to cure a variety of other complaints. Though all was done in Christ's name, it was a long time before the conviction that age old magic was also at work faded.

The same stubborn dualism long survived at two holy wells near Penzance. At *St. Maddern's Well*, visitors who have negotiated the several stiles to reach it, even today follow the ancient ritual of leaving a torn strip of clothing on the adjacent thorn bushes. In the past, it also was visited by mothers with sick children, who engaged their in a ceremony more linked to sun worship than to Christianity. Close to the well is the ruined baptistry, where, even today, there is the occasional baptism by local clergymen.

Of neighbouring *St. Ludgvan's Well*, it was claimed that no parishioner baptised in its waters would ever be hanged, and there seems to be no proof otherwise. In very ancient times the water was believed to cure all diseases afflicting the eye. Then, according to tradition, St. Ludgvan banished to the Red Sea a malignant spirit that had been plaguing the parish. As it fled, it spitefully spat in the well, cancelling its opthalmic efficacy!

The Well That Never Was

There is a difference between tradition, however shaky, and pure invention. In quite a few publications you might find a reference to the '*Well of St. Ruth.*' This began with mischievous students of the erstwhile Redruth School of Art, who, long ago 'pulled the leg' of their Principal with the story of the Well of St. Ruth, and of the appearance from time to time of the apparition of the saint dressed in a red robe. They added that this was how the town got its name. The gentleman put the story into a book, without checking that there was such a saint, and the error has been self perpetuating as equally careless writers copied it.

For other books on Cornwall, its heritage and culture, write to:

Dyllansow Truran
Trewolsta. Trewirgie
Redruth, Cornwall